REVELATIONS

Revelations

Gay Men's Coming-Out Stories

edited by
Adrien Saks & Wayne Curtis

Boston ◆ Alyson Publications, Inc.

FOR CHRISTOPHER A. TUTTLE
my stalwart, best friend
—A.S.

FOR TIM K.
Coming out is usually painful,
but always worthwhile.
—W.C.

Published as a trade paperback original by Alyson Publications, Inc.,
40 Plympton Street, Boston, Massachusetts 02118.
Distributed in England by GMP Publishers,
P.O. Box 247, London N17 9QR, England.

First edition: October 1988
Second edition: January 1994

ISBN 1-55583-244-X

5 4 3 2 1

Contents

Introduction

T he first person I came out to was my freshman roommate at Boston University. I only told him that I was gay because he told me that he was, first. It didn't seem fair for me to hold out when he had been so courageous. Despite my many fears, I stepped forward.

I remember thinking at the time that the words "I am gay" summed up so much of who I was, even though I had never kissed a man, read a gay book, or seen a movie with any gay characters. Still, being gay was somehow central to my life. Telling my roommate that I was gay communicated a lifetime of secret fears and dreams.

Editing this anthology has reconnected me to those difficult "before" years. Years of self-doubt and confusion. *Revelations* is an offering to the men who are in that stage today, struggling to leave their closets. This is your community, relating its experiences so that you might better find your way to us.

Revelations, as originally edited by Wayne Curtis, was published in 1988. For this new edition, I have substituted many new stories, and, where possible, I have updated information on the original contributors. I had several priorities in preparing this work. I wanted to preserve the level of diversity that Wayne had achieved with the first edition, focus on the quality of writing, and eliminate pseudonyms. In cases where I was unable to acquire permission to use real names, I have dropped stories that were in the previous edition. There is no room for anonymity in an anthology of coming-out stories. Not in 1994.

John Primavera and M.A. Williams, whose stories were originally published under the names Len Clumic and Phillip Mulhollin, both asked that their real names be used in future editions. I am happy to comply with their wishes.

As gay men, we are too often denied role models in our lives. There are few examples of out gay men in the public eye for us to emulate, and we are left to ourselves to answer the question "How do I live my life as an out gay man?" The writers in this anthology have grappled with that very question. I hope their stories will encourage and enlighten.

—Adrien Saks

Michael Lassell

The Summer of '65

It was one of those summers, slow and liquid, the grass as dark as green bottles, the nights still as stone. I still don't know what possessed me. The quiet of it all, perhaps. Or maybe it was finally time to just be myself, if only for a moment.

I'd known Ralph all my life. We went to different schools but attended the same Lutheran church. He was four years older and everything a boy ought to be in the eyes of every mother, which is to say, nothing like me.

His last name was Manners, and his were perfect. He was athletic, talented, outgoing, easy in himself. I was a fat sissy kid who liked art and music and felt awkward at any activity more physical than standing upright. To Ralph, a swimming pool was a plaything; for me it was a minefield of potential disaster.

We were not friends as children. I watched him from across the enormous gulf of four school-age years. He sang in the choir, as I did. He put a sheet on his head for the annual Christmas pageant, as I did, both of us pretending to be shepherds in costumes Mrs. Hutner and Mrs. Born made. But that was the extent of our shared existence.

In fact, it was probably not necessary for me to "come out" at all. I mean, who was going to be surprised? I was a classic homo in the making, if you happened to know what a homo was. But who even knew the stereotypes in those days of Norman Rockwell and *Father Knows Best*? Suburban children in the 1950s had limited access to information about sex, accurate or not, but somehow the rudiments managed to be shared.

Judy Deutsch and Leila Greif — who showed me theirs for a peek at mine — explained the approximate reality of menstruation to me at the age of nine or so, but I didn't believe their story. It seemed far too incongruous. Further forbidden facts of life were filled in during recess baseball games, so we all had a notion of the mechanics of procreation by the time we were ten or so. I always felt I knew less than everyone else, though — perhaps because I was always way out in deep right field, far away from the exchange of information.

If my classmates managed to acquire any knowledge about homosexuals, they never tipped their hand. They kept their distance, but it was not, I think, because they thought there was anything nefarious about my sexuality. We hadn't yet assimilated the vocabulary of hatred. In retrospect, having heard the horror stories other gay men tell, I'm grateful for the ignorance. I don't recall being called queer, or homo, or faggot — all words we just did not know.

I assume that I was not tortured for my utter difference from other kids primarily because I had a notorious temper that put people on guard. Awkward as I was, I was big, possibly even strong. And however different, I was a known entity: I'd been there since kindergarten, and I was included to the extent that I would consent to the will of the majority (a very limited extent, as my third-grade teacher told my mother, while I sat writing my first poem instead of going out to play).

Everyone knew I would shrink from missiles hurled my way on the playing fields, but in those milk-and-cookie days of Dwight D. Eisenhower, their shaming commentary never shifted into taunts of sexual deviance. I'm sure if Woody, Flop, and the others had known that queers existed, and what they were, they would have assumed me to be one, such being the rigors of stereotypes in those black-and-white sitcom days when conformity was a national pathology (as it has once again become).

It was at age ten or so that I first experienced sex, or at least libido, or at least that sickening, thrilling sensation in the groin that came to define me in the eyes of society. It was the first day in gym class in fifth grade, the first time we had to change clothes for a specific thing called Phys. Ed. Before, we'd always gone out to recess in what we'd worn to school.

I can picture the moment as if it were yesterday: the angle of my vision, the arrangement of gray lockers, my intense curiosity, the clumsy movements Jack made as he slipped out of his tan chinos down to his white Jockey shorts. All Jockey shorts were white in the '50s. I must have been paralyzed for a moment, fixated as I was on what was going on behind those briefs. Since I was an only child, I don't think I'd ever seen another penis before – except once, and that was my father's (which is another story altogether).

It would not be until two years later, the first day of gym class in junior high, at age twelve or so, that we were required to change out of underwear into jockstraps. And that's when I saw the first naked boy of my recollection. His name was George Bowen. He was one of the few black kids in my school, and he had the hard, muscled body of an adolescent about to become a very sexy man, a gymnast, in fact, in the days when all gymnasts were white, too. As I watched him strip, I kept wondering if his penis would be the same dark eggplant color of his skin. And when he stepped unself-consciously out of his underwear, I found out.

If seeing Jack in his underwear was my first experience with something called sexuality, it being an accident of gender segregation that it was *homo*sexuality, then seeing George Bowen naked was my first experience with desire. It was not, of course, my last. Nor, you may rest assured, my last experience with unrequited desire.

About this time Ralph and I were on a church basketball team together. My father was the coach. Ashamed of my fat and my prepubescent penis, I would refuse to shower with the older boys. But I did fall irrevocably in love with the hollows at the top of Ralph's thighs, alongside his perfect boy buttocks. This was, to be sure, the moment when an orientation became an identity, even though I did not know it at the time.

If I'd had an older brother, a cousin, or even a friend close enough to confide in, I might not have been as tormented about sex, or about being gay, as I was. But I did not. My church told me sex was wrong until marriage, that even masturbation was a sin, and that the wages of sin were everlasting torment. Jesus and I came to a parting of the ways, although I spent many later years looking for a lover who looked just like him.

I dated girls in those junior and senior high school years, although I had fierce crushes: one on a boy named Donald who is now a gay adult friend, another on an actor named Ray, whom I also still cherish, despite his cogent heterosexuality. But in those days I was still celibate and clueless. I left high school a virgin, and I was as ashamed of that as I was of my increasingly conscious predilection for boys. I am furious now to know that many boys were having sex with each other back then, that many – both hetero- and homosexual – were regularly experimenting with sex. I was retarded in this area and knew it.

And so I graduated from Great Neck South one June day of 1965. My parents, whom I detested by then, had refused to let me take a girl named Linda to the senior prom because she was black. I was already in the civil rights movement in those days (in the most tentative way); my parents were, and I believe still are, bigots of the most unextraordinary, casual kind. They are white and Christian and see no reason the rest of the world shouldn't be too.

I was also, by the summer of 1965, drinking – routinely and alone. At night I would go to bars around the neighborhood and sit with the fathers and grandfathers of kids I knew, drinking beers faster than any of them, even the ones who eventually died of cirrhosis. I was as lonely as anyone gets, and I was headed for disaster.

How Ralph came back into my life at that point remains a mystery, or why we became friends. Maybe it was the changing times, maybe it was the kindness of his all-American heart.

Ralph was in college in upstate New York, at one of the mediocre public universities. He was working for the summer at Kennedy Airport, which had only recently been renamed after the 1963 assassination of the president. He was unloading airplane sewage containers into tank trucks until midnight. He was living at his parents' house, a few blocks away from my own. Eventually I came to be waiting for him.

Now, I should say at this point that I have been searching for a brother all my life. As a teenager, I discovered my father's condoms one day and poked pinholes in one, hoping to engineer an unplanned sibling. I failed. My closest friendships still most resemble the bonding of two loving brothers, and any story about brothers in conflict, fact or fiction, starts adrenaline pumping through my system. Even the notion of discord between brothers makes me hyperventilate. The Civil War, with its tales of brother-against-brother fighting, makes me weep (Stephen Crane's *The Red Badge of Courage,* for example). It is clear to me now that Ralph was the brother I was looking for. I trusted him.

We'd sit around a lot, Ralph and I, having the kind of conversations boys have on their way to becoming men: sometimes deep, often silly, more important in the time they take than in their content. We even went on a double date once. He was surprised I was not the "goody two-shoes" I had been as a child; I was surprised he was more of a hellion than I had imagined. We both had a rebel streak that had been hidden for a long time.

It was because Ralph played guitar when he was in high school (Kingston Trio stuff mostly, Chad Mitchell Trio, early acceptable folk music) that I took up the six strings. And by the summer of 1965, we were strumming along together. He taught me most of what I've long forgotten, including the chords to the classic anti-war song, "Johnny, We Hardly Knew Ya," which Joan Baez had shortly before raised to new artistic heights.

As a boy who was rejected routinely by other boys and men, a boy who had been raised in the company of doting women, including a mother who welded me to her with wrought-iron apron strings, I basked in the sunlight of Ralph's attention. I felt *liked* for the first time in my life. The first time he just arrived at the house to see me, as if that were the most natural thing in the world, I felt as if my life might have possibilities after all.

I look back on all of this and think, Could it all have happened in one summer? Time went so slowly in those days, and I was so impatient. Within a week, the world could change. It did: I turned eighteen.

That Saturday night, my closest family friend, Linda (who is four years older and a contemporary, therefore, of Ralph's), took me to a movie and dinner. Then we sat on the lawn and waited for Ralph to return from the airport. The three of us drove off to a bar and got roaring drunk, ordering drafts by the dozen, and we blasted ourselves giddy on a trio of kazoos on the way home in Ralph's BMW convertible. It was the best of times. I passed out on Ralph's parents' living room floor (they were away).

When I came to, I threw up, looked around the house, then headed out into the July night. It was early Sunday morning, still dark but warm as day. I was wearing shorts and had no idea where my sandals were. I was sitting in the middle of an empty intersection, on a manhole cover, tossing a Dixie ice cream cup cover up and down when my father turned into the street, the headlights of his car catching me from a hundred yards away. My mother was hysterical, he informed me; he was furious. Inside, he found Linda in bed with Ralph. It was a family crisis of the highest magnitude. In my parents' eyes, only Ralph seemed blameless. Linda and I were subject to all the humiliations of tyrannical parents too foolish to know normal behavior when they see it, too normal to know extraordinary behavior when they see it, and making no allowances whatsoever for individual expression – a term that hadn't yet been coined.

July melted away, and August rolled around, which meant September separation was just around the corner. Ralph would be off to graduate school, I to Colgate for the first of four loathsome years in a transparent closet. We were sitting on the Little League field off Marcus Avenue in New Hyde Park about two o'clock one morning. I guess Ralph loved the place – he'd had success there, such acclaim. I'd never been there that I could remember, but in the middle of the night, in the days before Little League fields were fenced in and padlocked after dark, I felt just fine, safe, at home.

The grass was still warm, I remember, and only a bit damp. I have no idea how the conversation got around to it, but at one point Ralph brought up the topic – or the word – homosexuality.

"I think that's what I am," I said, with only the slightest hesitation.

Ralph paused for a moment. "How do you know?" he asked.

"I just do," I said.

"Have you ever had sex with a man?" he wanted to know.

"No."

"A woman?"

"No."

"Then how do you know?" There wasn't any accusation in it. He was actually curious, interested in the answer.

"I'm not sure. It's just the way I feel about boys. I don't feel that way about girls."

I don't know if Ralph ever wondered if I felt desire for him, which, of course, I did. If it occurred to him, he never spoke of it.

"Well," he said, "my advice is, try it first with a girl."

He spent the rest of the summer trying, vainly, to present me with the opportunity.

And so it was that I came out to the first person in my life, the most important person in my life at the time, this young heterosexual brother of a man who was my friend. He continued to be my friend, as accepting of my sexuality as he was of my fledgling political beliefs. As things turned out, I did not follow his advice. I started having sex of the most tentative kind with other students at Colgate, which was then an all-male bastion of middle-class mendacity (a word I learned there). I had sex with girls, too, as we called young women in those prefeminist days. I even started to know other men who acknowledged they were gay. By the winter of my sophomore year, I had a friend named Robert Lowe who shared his own darkest secret with me. I was the first person he ever told he was gay. A circle felt complete, but happiness did not abound.

I became a pot head. This was, after all, the '60s. I took other drugs, I got into theater, I became an anti-war leftist, an honor student, a drunk. Ralph and I grew gradually apart, as he finally submitted to the government's call. As an ROTC graduate, he went off to officer training school and was commissioned as an air force lieutenant and a pilot. When Robert and I went off to study drama in London in 1968, Ralph went to Vietnam. He never came home. His plane was shot down and he was reported missing in action along with his flight crew, all presumed dead.

Robert, who eventually became an attorney specializing in adoptions, died of AIDS in New York City in 1991. His mother reported to the *New York Times* and the Colgate alumni newsletter that her son had died of a heart attack. For this lie she is never to be forgiven.

◆

In the summer of 1993, I remember the summer of 1965 as an endless progression of deep feelings and shooting stars. One vast cloudless night, Ralph and I were talking about God.

Since we knew each other from a fundamentalist church, the talk was fairly radical. It was his belief that one first accepts the received religion of one's parents unquestioningly, that one then rejects religion entirely and pursues a path of doubt, and eventually comes to a personal understanding of God on one's own terms.

That has, in fact, been the shape of my own stumbling spiritual journey, my attempt to find God in a world in which the evidence of his nonexistence is overwhelming.

In a sense, I feel that the process of coming out is similar. First, one comes out to oneself. In my case, that meant finding out what homosexuality was and where I fit on the continuum of hetero-to-homoeroticism (I'd found out about Kinsey when I researched a health class report in tenth grade). Then I had to come out to others, one at a time, sometimes in groups. My first appearance at a public gay event was the first pride march in 1970. Then one makes being out a part of one's own personal adjustment to life, and being out becomes less about being politically correct than about being true to one's heart.

There are other stories I could tell about coming out. I actually enjoy some of the ironies, now, many years later. At the time, they caused considerable anguish.

When I told my parents I was gay, in the angriest possible way, at age twenty-four, they said that my sixth-grade teacher had told them I would be gay when I was twelve. That might have been helpful information during the decade I was suicidal about them finding out. Their adjustment has been slow and imperfect.

When I was one of the chairpersons of the New Haven Gay Liberation Front in the early '70s, I was having a torrid romance with my lesbian co-chair, a peaches-and-cream-complected Vassar medievalist. No one could figure out if we were avant-garde or hideously corrupt, and so, absent either consensus or coherent theory, we floundered around until inertia and LSD led us apart.

In the early '80s, now clean, sober, and seriously involved with a lover named Ben, I was asked when applying for a job, how I spent my spare time. I responded with uncharacteristic honesty that I was an alcoholic in recovery and that I spent a lot of my evenings at meetings. I told my prospective employer that I was on the board of a recovery house for gay and lesbian alcoholics and drug addicts, and that I was the secretary of the lesbian and gay Stonewall Democratic Club of Los Angeles. Because this potential boss was looking for someone with a sense of commitment in his/her life, he hired me on the spot. I have been out at work ever since, although I have had many intervening jobs.

◆

And so, in this ongoing process, I came out again at the March on Washington on April 25, 1993. I went with my friend Matt, who is young enough to be both the brother and son I never had, and someone I loved rather more thoroughly than I should, given his nonreciprocity. At some point before the march, we walked over to the Lincoln Memorial and then to the adjacent Vietnam Veterans Memorial.

In a crowd that was almost exclusively queer, I led Matt to Ralph's named, etched primly in the polished stone. I could see the two of us in the reflection. Walking away from RALPH W. MANNERS, I began to cry. It's hard not to. Matt took my hand and let me weep.

It was not just for Ralph I was crying, of course, but for Robert and all my other dear, dead friends who have succumbed to AIDS: soul mate Kenny, kindest Clark, and my first lover, Roberto, who came out one day to his immigrant mother and sister because he loved me so much he didn't care if they rejected him. And I cried, too, for my isolated youth, and for the isolation of all those heartland brothers and sisters who cannot come out, and for the sailors beaten to death in foreign countries by homophobic shipmates, and for lesbian officers drummed out of the army and out of the families, and even for Leonard Matlovich, the decorated Vietnam veteran activist I never particularly liked, who said of the military, "They gave me a medal for killing two men and a discharge for loving one."

And in that weeping I came out again. Because how much more out can we be, each of us one among many millions, than to reach into the silent, secret places of our souls and to face life with all the untidy, graceless emotions flying like rainbow flags, and to reach out to another gay being, who offers love and support, and to feel the ancient hurt and the radiating love, the unhealed shame and the salving joy, and a pride so enormous it transcends banners and slogans? How much more out can we be? How much more human?

Steve Nohava

My Discovery of Me

My name is Steve Nohava. I was born on February 4, 1970. Until I was eleven, most of my life had been spent running around the U.S. with an alcoholic mother and a father who kept abandoning us. I lost five years of school, but I managed to learn about the world by reading brochures, books, and newspapers. I usually bore the brunt of my mother's behavior when she got drunk, since I was always around and my dad wasn't. We would argue; she'd throw beer bottles at me, hit me with a garden hoe, and often abandon me.

By June of 1981, I had been through thirty-one states. I began to wonder how I could ever make anything of myself if I continued to miss school and subject myself to my parents' continued abuse and neglect. Slowly but surely, I started wanting to get away from that life, and I began to think of ways to do so.

My chance came on a sunny day in late July. My mother and I were in downtown Norfolk at a city bus shelter. We were waiting for a bus when she suddenly gave me five dollars and said, "Take this and go see if there are any movies here. If not, come back."

I looked for fifteen minutes or so all over the downtown area, but I didn't find a single movie theater. When I got back to the bus stop, my mother was not there.

I immediately said to myself, "I am sick and tired of being neglected, abused, and abandoned just so my mother can continue to drink. I desperately need to try a different life. I give my mother exactly one hour to show up. If she doesn't, I will walk to that pay phone across the street, dial 911, and turn myself in to the police."

The hour slowly went by with no word from my mother. I walked to the phone, dialed 911, and when the man said, "Norfolk Police," I said:

"My name is Steve Nohava. My mother abandoned me at the Granby Mall bus stop. She has done this to me several times before. I want to turn myself in to the police and start a new life."

Within minutes a cop car showed up, and I went with them. I told them all that had happened in my life. I was told that I would be put in the custody of social services. I was in a shelter home until the courts put me in the custody of Chesapeake Social Services in August.

While I was in the shelter, I had my first gay experience. Mark and I were roommates throughout my stay there. One day, while we were taking a nap, Mark climbed up to the top bunk and lay beside me. I didn't pay any mind. Then he moved his hand to my crotch and massaged me. He asked, "Do you mind?"

I replied, "No, it's okay." It felt so good, I began to get a hard-on. We massaged each other, and sucked each other off. We were both thoroughly pleased with this contact, and I asked Mark if we could do it again.

He replied, "Yes, whenever you want."

So we continued our "sessions of contact," as we called them, every night and every day at naptime. It was a sad moment when it came time to hug good-bye. We left the shelter on the same day; me to a foster home, Mark to his real home. We didn't have time to get each other's address. I will always remember him, for he helped me have the best moments of my life.

I began to notice I was different soon after I was put into foster and group homes in October of 1981. I saw people call each other "fairy," "homo," "fag," and "queer" simply because they were patting each other on the shoulder. I saw this in other teenagers and even some adults. I knew nothing about these words, but since I didn't do any name-calling, I got teased, too.

I found that the only way to be safe from the harassment was to start showing interest in the opposite sex and have a girlfriend. I rejected that idea immediately, since I did not see what was so special about females. I had enjoyed my encounters with Mark.

The pressure of feeling and acting different began to mount. I looked up *homo, faggot,* and the other words in the dictionary and encyclopedia. Some I couldn't find; others were defined as "slang for homosexual." I turned to *homosexual* and *homosexuality.* The definition read, "A person attracted to members of the same sex or gender."

I couldn't believe that my peers and some adults put down homosexuals just because they exist. I had never rejected the idea of men enjoying the contact I had. I heard the news talk dirty about gays. Others mentioned how disgusting "it" was. Gays were often the objects of jokes. Even the church talked about how much of a sin gayness was. I could not find any books that didn't talk about homosexuality as a disease or a psychiatric disorder that should be treated. I felt that I was caught between my perfectly normal feelings and a homophobic society.

During the two years I was gathering this information, I felt there was no one to turn to. Once I saw this society for what it was, I could do nothing but cry, because I feared I had to face ridicule, rejection, and loneliness because I performed sexual acts with men. I tried soul-searching and prayer for a "cure." But I still had my deep desires for other guys.

In November of 1984, things began to turn around for me when I moved to a group home in northern Virginia. I had a counselor there who seemed open-minded and comforting. She noticed I was down in the dumps one day and asked what was wrong. I replied, "I'm not sure how you will take this, but I think you are open-minded enough to hear it. I think I might very well be a homosexual."

She said, "Okay. To me it wouldn't matter if the whole world was gay, but right now only ten percent of us are. Tell me, how did you come to this conclusion?"

I was totally shocked! Never before had I seen anyone react so calmly and reassuringly to what I thought was a crisis. I went ahead and took up over an hour telling her my life story.

She told me that she found my life very interesting because she had had similar problems. Finally she said, "I have to go to a meeting now, but here are a couple of books I think will help you." She reached into her briefcase and pulled out two books: one entitled *One Teenager in Ten* and another called *Gays among Us*.

I began to read them immediately. I felt reassured after reading the stories and knowing that the people who wrote them went through the same problems I did, and they found ways to press on in life. I no longer felt lonely. And I began to gain more wisdom and courage.

My counselor gave me permission to use the order form in the back of *One Teenager in Ten* to order more books. I imme-diately ordered *Young, Gay and Proud!* and several others. I read them as soon as they arrived. I was pleased and amazed to find information that I had not seen before, like "Gays have been around since Ancient Greece," and plenty of others. The biggest message I got was GAY IS GOOD! I gained so much confidence and started liking myself. I wanted to write this new discovery on walls!

I also got two pen pals in February 1985 through a correspondence center at the same time I placed my book order. These friends gave me more information, support, encouragement, and praise. We still write each other and have developed a very strong bond.

Not long after I got the books, I had to deal directly with anti-gay violence and name-calling. The other kids had seen the title *Young, Gay and Proud!* on one of the books. The news went all through the home like wildfire. Before the week was out, I got teased, harassed, and got two black eyes.

The group home pressed assault-and-battery charges against the kid who gave me the black eyes. I had to testify in court against him. When he got up on the stand, the judge asked him why he had hit me.

"Because he is a homosexual," he answered.

The judge responded, "Poor excuse for anybody. You need to learn how to control your temper. I sentence you to Barret Correctional Center, where they will teach you a thing or two. I authorize any length of time deemed necessary. Case closed."

I wrote my pen pals to ask for their advice on how to handle the name-calling. They suggested three solutions: (1) ignore it, (2) stay away from the problem, and (3) say a creative phrase in return, such as "Thank you for the compliment. Have a nice day, baby!" I didn't have a problem following the advice, but when I used the creative phrases, some of the kids could not keep their cool. They cursed at me and threatened me, but they ended up getting restrictions.

In May 1985, my counselor friend got a new job and left the group home. We hugged each other for a long time — until I stopped crying — and I thanked her for all her support and guidance. She told me, "I helped you get a start. You are doing an excellent job. Now you must go seek your new friends and life. Take good care."

In November of that year, I moved to a new group home. By that time my parents, the service agency, and the staff at the new home knew all about my gayness. The staff accepted me and were very supportive. My parents don't discuss it.

It wasn't long before word got out among the other kids that I was gay. The whole issue led to a group meeting where several people asked me if the rumors were true. I said, "Yes. I am gay and proud of it."

For a while I had to put up with a lot of name-calling and ignorance. I ignored most of it, but when it started to be an annoyance or when they hit me, I went to the staff. They were always very understanding and supportive, and usually gave the troublemakers a restriction or punishment of some sort. When the staff were not available, I used my creative phrases, like "You don't know what you are missing!" or "You ought to try it. It might be good for you." That really threw them.

After I turned sixteen, things began to cool out. I have had few, if any, problems with other residents bothering me. Some of the main troublemakers have been discharged from here, so those who continue picking on me have little support from anyone else. I have even had some kids come up and talk to me about my gayness. I talked to them honestly and openly, and I did not hesitate to answer their questions. Now, instead of picking fights, we go our separate ways. For me, GAY IS GOOD!

Robert Friedman

Creation Myth

(First-Husband Story)

The liberal son of a liberal father and mother, I never had much trouble coming out to myself. It wasn't, as my first heart-stopping boyfriend would have it, that I came out of the womb singing "Glad to Be Gay," but once I figured out I was as bent as they come, I figured I may as well enjoy it.

My first dabbling in sex was with two other precocious boys in the neighborhood. Unfortunately, soon after our initial forays into group groping, creating a rotating sex club in one another's basements, we were closed down. My family moved to a new state, ostensibly because of my father's new position on the faculty of a college in Baltimore. I always figured I was somehow responsible for the shake-up by my flagrant sex play, though.

Fortunately, I was blessed with a father who, through some miracle of old-world manners, had no problem with public displays of affection between us, hugging and kissing me upon reunions at airports and train terminals with no fear of male disapproval. In some ways being Jewish, a lifelong Leftie, an intellectual, and an academic had already alienated him from mainstream American norms. I will always be grateful to my father for making it so easy for me to grow into loving men. In some ways he was the perfect Homosexual's Father, the kind who might come in a kit. He even loved opera, show music, and boxing. My grandfather was a bantamweight prize-fighter in New York City; I figure this, too, is a good pedigree for a homosexual. (Pugilism, the play of male bodies, involving punishing blows and buckets of sweat, has always seemed to me peculiarly homoerotic.)

From both parents, Jack and Irene, I got my love of books. I was always scouring the stacks at the library for some mention in print of gay boys, but this was a thirst which mostly went unquenched. Meanwhile, my mother was the first to encourage me in my literary aspirations; all through my adolescence I wrote stories, poetry, and plays.

Still, I feared my parents' reaction, should they discover I was gay. There's the rub in all of this liberal enlightenment: despite my family's free-thinking ideology, we did not live in a vacuum, and America's evil homophobia came seeping in. I remember my dad joking with a buddy about being hit on by "homos." My sister warned me when my outfit looked "faggy." So I didn't come out; I went away to college instead.

At Penn I could enjoy gay dances and the then-fascinating world of Philly gay bars and discos. I had flukey, half-assed romances with other college boys and an occasional chef, all unbeknownst to my family far away — psychologically, at least — in suburban Maryland.

There was less than two hours' drive-time between us, however, so it was inevitable that I'd incriminate myself somehow. When I was eventually found out, I could only blame a lapse of vigilance on my part, a sloppiness in deception which resulted from my weakness for Catholic boys.

◆

In the spring of my junior year, I ventured up to Provincetown to find a summer job in the famous fag resort. What I found instead, down the hall in my guest house, the S'il Vous Plait, was an incredibly fetching young man from New Hampshire named Larry. His curly-haired, good-time-boy looks pushed every eroto-attraction button in my circuitry, and we had soon given up the job search in favor of going at it in my tacky room. We were fueled by (I cringe to admit) gin and Orange Crush.

When I returned to P'town after finals, all of fifty dollars in my pocket, I worked as a houseboy at a guest house, which provided me my tiny, basement dungeon-room rent-free. Larry was bussing tables at the Cafe Blase. Soon I was doing the same at a fishhouse, which meant I could quit my slave quarters at the guest house and rent a love pad of my own on Commercial Street. "Awww, busboys in love," sniped an especially cynical waiter at my restaurant whenever he saw us, sweet puppies holding hands and strolling through the tourist town.

P'town is a strange phenomenon during the summer. Each ferry brings a load of day-trippers, inundating the streets until the boat leaves at the end of the day. Nighttime is given over to tourists, and the people who live in town to serve them.

The season brought with it, in a loveboat of their own, my sister and her young husband. Susan and Richard stayed in P'town long enough to be my guests at the Pied Piper, a lesbian dance bar which was being generous with gay men that year. At one point, the young marrieds danced alongside Larry and me to "Johnny, Are You Queer?" Still, it was not until they were on the long car ride back home that Susan turned to Richard and wondered aloud if maybe her younger brother were gay.

Their visit was actually the beginning of my coming out to my family — first in the form of letters, then in person. I declared my true self to my sister, brother, and cousin, all to generally good reviews. Perhaps the shock that they registered was feigned for my benefit, but it wore off quickly.

Alas, summer must end, and with it, summer romance. Not content with embodying a cliche, I implored Larry to come live with me during my senior year at Penn. I was rooming with a lesbian who gradually seduced all of my women friends during fall semester. Our flat was the first floor of a converted brothel, complete with blood red carpeting, mahogany fireplaces, and huge sliding French doors between rooms. There was more than enough room in my huge bedroom for the gorgeosity which was due to arrive on a plane from Boston.

From the time he opened his hazel-blue eyes under the tousled locks in the morning, to the time he lay his lithe, finely muscled body down at night, Larry's young, virile beauty completely enthralled me — which of course was a ridiculous and hopeless way to run a relationship. A recipe for sweetheart disaster. But that is another story.

Eventually, my parents decided to surprise their son and treat him to brunch by driving up to Philadelphia on a bright Sunday morning. That morning, we were awakened by the doorbell at an unholy hour: ten o'clock. Larry grunted and rolled over onto his side attractively. I threw on a nightshirt and went to answer the door, thinking it must be one of my insatiable roomie's womyn friends. I didn't bother to slide shut the bedroom doors; the handsome thing inside sprawled nude on the coverlet like a beefcake greeting card, *Wish you were here.*

Imagine my surprise when Irene and Jack strolled into my little world, making promises of brunch and stopping cold when confronted with the erotic tableau framed by the open bedroom doors. The boyfriend sprang up wildly to cover himself; I wheeled the heavy doors together. *Pay no attention to the man behind the curtain.*

Still in shock at having seen what warmed my sheets, the parents retreated as far from the bedroom doors as possible, snooping around the living room in a manner that pretended indifference. Of course all of their antennae were out. I hadn't had time to defag the flat, so Irene spotted a cover of *Christopher Street* which asked the pointed question, "Are You a Gay Preppie?" (I was. Today, after ten years on the Left Coast, determinedly downwardly mobile, I am not.) It was a photo of a cheerful specimen in blue blazer and hornrims, the identifying features painstakingly labeled. "Robert," my mother asked, "what is this?"

"Just a magazine cover," I said, trying to affect nonchalance. I willed myself to see the artifact with my mother's eyes. She was puzzled, no doubt, that impeccable attention to dress and grooming — traits she'd raised me to consider important, after all — could indicate sexual perversion. It was as if some New York magazine had chosen its cover story specifically to indict her.

"Never mind," she said, the martyred tone which echoed throughout my childhood creeping into her voice. *"I don't want to know."*

Just then the French doors slid open to reveal Larry, all boyish charm in my bathrobe. "Good morning, Mr. and Mrs. Friedman," he said winningly.

Brunch, at the Knave of Hearts on South Street, moved at a glacial pace, burdened by a host of unanswered questions and what my psychologist friend calls "willful ignorance." Larry, love of my puppy life, fire of my puppy loins, might have been a waiter sitting at the table to tally his checks, so impersonally did my parents treat him. Noticing that both my father and I sopped up our bowls of mushroom bisque with crusts of bread, Larry remarked genially, "That's so Old World of you!"

Jack peered at him through the top of his bifocals. "And where do your ancestors come from, young man?"

"French Canada," Larry admitted, the blush starting at his temples and spreading down to his perfect neck. "I guess I come from the Old Country, too." This was the high point of the meal, at the end of which my folks returned to the I-95 corridor, leaving my man and me to our raided love nest. They never dropped in on me, unexpectedly, again.

◆

I like to say that I've had four husbands, which, at the ripe old age of thirty-two, makes me feel like Zsa Zsa Gabor. To my parents' credit, each successive "lover" has met with more live, humanlike interaction. When the 'rents came to San Francisco to visit me, I decided they needed immersion therapy in fag culture. I took them to see *Don Giovanni* at the Castro Theatre. It was Irene, Jack, every opera queen in the city, and I, for three full hours, hugging, crying, and shrieking. At the time, I was together with Peter, and before my folks left, Jack took him aside and said: "Take good care of my boy." I was very touched by that.

With the fabulous Doug Rose, cordiality gave way to outright admiration. It helped that Doug had won a $30,000 undergraduate prize and a Fulbright scholarship, with which he was taking me to Europe. My parents know from good husband material.

And the extraordinary Dean Decent bowled them over to such an extent that, preferring fantasy to reality, my father insisted that Dean's electric red hair indicated he must be a member of the long-lost tribe of Israel.

Dad died a few years ago, but my mom has gamely tried to keep up with me. Susan and Richard have children who are getting to know what it's like having an unabashed queer uncle. When they're old enough, I'll encourage them to come out to California to visit and let their hair down a bit from that civilized Right Coast upbringing.

Robin, my Penn roommate, used to say that our coming-out stories are our creation myths, the places in our life-narratives where we begin re-inventing ourselves as modern homosexuals. This is mine, and if there is some "whoops" and some "what the hell" in it, so goes my life as well.

Larry Duplechan

Birthday Present

A reminiscence

Among the Acknowledgments at the beginning of my second novel, *Blackbird,* is one that reads: "Larry R., for the best eighteenth birthday present a kid ever got." This is the story of that present.

It was Saturday, December 30, 1974. Gerald R. Ford was president. "Lucy in the Sky with Diamonds" by Elton John was number one with a bullet on the Billboard pop charts. It was the best of times. It was the worst of times. It was my eighteenth birthday. I was at work.

I was just another eighteen-year-old black gay college freshman at UCLA, helping to meet the high cost of my higher education by working part-time at the McDonald's in Westwood Village (in those days a bustling college town; in these days one of the world's largest shopping malls, with a major university quite inexplicably attached to it, like an appendix). Bachelor's degrees were expensive, even then.

I worked the grill, flipping Big Macs, frying fries, secretly sampling dill pickle slices. I bore the scars of a thousand grease burns from my wrists to my armpits, and on those days when I'd dash from school down Westwood Boulevard to the Golden Arches to put in a couple of quick hours between classes, I invariably returned to campus with ketchup behind my ears, smelling mighty like a Quarter Pounder with cheese.

More than once the store manager – a scruffy walrus of a man named Bill with a penchant for loud, fat neckties and too much Brut after-shave – had offered me a cashier gig, which would have afforded me a bit more money and far fewer grease burns. I'd refused. Not because I enjoyed working the grill (would a snowman enjoy a summer in Miami?) but because even though, as an English lit major, I had read *Beowulf* and understood most of it, and could recite from memory the first several stanzas of the Prologue to the *Canterbury Tales* in a better-than-average Middle English accent, and despite an embarrassingly high IQ, a current 3.75 grade point average, and a lightning wit, I could not make change. Not at gunpoint. Still can't.

Anyway – on that Saturday afternoon some forty-eight hours shy of 1975, I was lowering a basket of frozen apple pies into a bubbling deep-fat vat, only half-cognizant of the two or three other grill workers chattering away in Spanish (I was the only person on the grill team born north of the Mexican border), when I was startled by a surreptitious tickle to my lower ribcage. I turned quickly and looked into the grinning face of our district manager, Robert. (Actually, Robert was not his real name. His real name was Larry. And my name is Larry. And two guys named Larry in one small story could get a trifle confusing. So we'll call him Robert, okay?)

Robert was thirty years old – I'd asked. He had butch-cut blond hair and pale blue eyes and an infectiously boyish grin that never failed to make me want to bite my lip. It was a Mickey-Rooney-as-Andy-Hardy grin crossed with what I would years later term the *Mandate*-centerfold fuck-you grin.

"Hey, big Larry," Robert said in his testosterone-laced bedroom-basso voice. Robert liked to call me "big Larry" — a small joke, as I've never been what you'd call a large person. He tossed me another grin.

I saw his grin, and raised him a giggle and a quick, breathy "Hi."

"So what's new?" Robert pretended to adjust the oversized collar of my oversized blue work smock. He stood so close I could smell his cologne, even over the all-pervasive smell of junk food.

"Today's my birthday," I said. "I'm eighteen today." I had to look up a little to meet Robert's eyes. We were really just about the same height, but I was wearing Hush Puppies, and Robert was wearing shoes with two-inch heels. Very cool shoes in 1974. He was also wearing a beige double-knit suit — very cool threads in 1974 — and his trim, small-waisted body did quite well by it.

"Well," Robert said, "happy birthday."

"So what are you going to give me?" I smiled what I hoped was a playfully seductive smile.

Robert paused a moment, and grinned another one of those grins.

"Not to worry," he said finally. "We'll think of something."

And he walked away, his high shoes clicking against the greasy floor. I watched his well-shouldered beige double-knit back moving away, and I wondered if Robert was going to give me what I wanted for my birthday.

I suppose now is as good a point as any to mention that as of the afternoon of my eighteenth birthday, I was a virgin. Purer than Ivory soap; untouched as the parsley garnish on a T-bone steak.

Which is not to say I hadn't known what I wanted for years. Because, believe me, I'd known. I'd acknowledged myself as gay at around the age of thirteen. I read the chapter on homosexuality in *Everything You've Always Wanted to Know about Sex,* and thought: *Yep, that's me all righty.* And I'd been falling madly, passionately, head-over-tuchus in love with a veritable parade of boys since Mike McCarthy unwittingly stole my twelve-year-old heart in the seventh grade. But as of that Saturday afternoon of December 30, 1974 — not counting masturbation (and let's just say I jerked off quite a lot and leave it at that) — I had never had sex.

Which is not to say I didn't really want to, because believe me, I really wanted to. It wasn't as if I'd had no offers, because in the four months or so since I'd left home for college, I'd had my share. I attended the Gay Students Union meetings at school every Tuesday night, quite undiscouraged by the fact that at the first meeting I'd attended, in a simple white t-shirt and 501s ensemble, I was almost immediately mistaken for a lesbian. *By* a lesbian. I hadn't started lifting weights yet.

Still, over several weeks' worth of meetings, I'd had offers. I was asked home by a smallish (but not entirely unattractive) bush-league poet wearing wire-rimmed eyeglasses with only one lens. I was approached by an overweight black man in his midfifties. (Now I don't want to get into a big age thing here, but my *father* was in his late forties at this point, okay?) A willowy blond who called himself Golden, in a pale pink shirt and about a hundred silver bracelets, informed me (in a lisp you could water your ficus with) that he was strongly attracted to the innate savagery of the black male, and I might have obliged him with whatever savagery I could muster — he was very pretty, after all — if it wasn't that I've always liked my men to be just a little more, well, manly. I was propositioned by a tall, dark, handsome Greek with shoulder-length hair, who invited me to spend the evening with him, his girlfriend, and a large jar of Miracle Whip. Not exactly how I'd envisioned my first time, y'know?

So, one thing and another, I was still a virgin. I mean, I'd waited this long, so why not hold out for someone halfway decent, right?

Then there was Robert. Good-looking and sexy and just old enough – a man of some experience, more than likely. And he liked me, this much was certain. Who better to relieve me of the ever more cumbersome burden of my virginity? Provided he was gay, of course, which I wasn't exactly sure of yet. I mean, how could I be sure? Sure, he smiled at me a lot, and winked at me. And tickled me. And patted my ass. Okay, I was pretty sure.

There was the time Robert found me in the walk-in refrigerator, taking inventory of frozen hamburger patties. Robert peeked in and said, "Boy, you could really freeze your balls off in there." Big pause while he lifted one golden eyebrow and grinned for me. "And we certainly wouldn't want *that!*"

There was the time Robert spotted me stacking brownies onto a big plastic platter and walked over to me, stood just close enough to make my skin prickle, and whispered into my ear, "Hello, little brownie."

And then of course, there was the historic Cut Finger Incident.

Two or three weeks before my birthday, after several weeks of smiles and tickles and winky-winky with Robert, I'd pulled the not exactly exciting task of refilling nonfood inventory, which consisted mostly of slicing open large corrugated cardboard cartons of various supplies (little packets of ketchup, boxes of coffee stirrers, those little containers your french fries come in — that sort of thing), and stacking these supplies on the shelves in the stock room. Fabulous, right?

So anyway, I'm upstairs in the stock room, slicing open these big boxes of, say, Filet-O-Fish sandwich wrappers with an Exacto knife, probably singing to myself (maybe "Lucy in the Sky with Diamonds"), when who should appear at the top of the staircase but Robert. Not having heard anyone come up the stairs, and momentarily startled by the sudden appearance of anybody (let alone Robert), my knife-wielding right hand slipped, slicing a very impressive gash in my left index finger. Very showy, lots of blood. Not very deep, though.

Now, I'm not real good with blood. My own, that is. Not that I get hysterical or anything. On the contrary: I tend to watch myself bleed with a sort of calm fascination, until I go into shock. So I'm just standing there, watching my finger spurt blood all over these Filet-O-Fish sandwich wrappers, when Robert says, "Dr. Robert to the rescue!"

He moved quickly to the first aid kit mounted on a nearby wall (the stock room was probably the scene of many an Exacto knife injury), and before I even had time to go into shock, Robert had blotted my blood with a cotton ball, spritzed my finger with Bactine, and wrapped it in a large ouchless Curad.

We just stood there for a moment: Robert holding my injured hand up between our faces, me staring past my wound and into Robert's blue eyes.

"You gonna be all right?" he asked.

I nodded.

"You want me to kiss it and make it all better?"

I nodded vigorously.

And you know what? The man actually kissed my finger. That was when I became — well — pretty sure Robert liked me. I mean really *liked* me.

So back to my birthday:

Shortly after I'd announced my birthday to Robert, he came walking back through the grill area. He stopped directly behind me where I stood shooting Big Mac sauce onto buns with a big sauce gun.

"Eighteen, huh?" he said to the back of my head.

"Yep."

"Hm. Street legal."

Street legal? Robert moved in a little closer.

"How about I give you a ride home after work today?" Robert whispered into the nape of my neck, making every hair on my body stand at attention.

"Okay."

For the remainder of my shift, I was largely incapable of work. I would have been hard pressed to recognize a hamburger in a room full of objects. A ride home. This, I thought to myself, was It.

And then things really start to blur. I, who pride myself on my astounding memory for detail, for being able to recall large swaths of my life with the crispness and clarity of a fine motion picture; I find I only remember the next hour or so in bits and pieces, like those smeared, blurry black-and-white photographs we used to take with Polaroid "Swinger" cameras.

I remember Robert steering me out the back door of the store, calling "Lunch!" over his shoulder to whomever, and my heart pounding like a jackhammer. I remember he drove me home in a white Corvette with red leather upholstery. I remember he stopped at a liquor store and bought a bottle of creme de Cassis and a large bag of Doritos. I remember he grabbed my thigh between gear shiftings, and my dick got so hard so fast I nearly blacked out.

We sat in the miniscule living area of the single apartment I shared with the sort of nonentity roommate that college life seems to inflict upon the best of us. Luckily, he worked Saturdays, too. And we ate tortilla chips and drank Cassis (which, to tell the truth, I don't much like), and we talked about ... something. Again, blur. But needless to say, you could have sliced, diced, crinklecut, and julienned the sexual tension in the room.

At one point, I got up to refill our glasses in the kitchen. I was standing at the kitchen counter, pouring the stuff, and when I turned around, a full glass in each hand, there was Robert. Right there where I'd turned, so we were practically nose to nose. And I went to hand Robert his glass, but he didn't take it. So I'm just standing there like a schmuck, holding a Cassis on the rocks in each hand, and just barely breathing, when Robert kissed me. Softly. Sweetly. On my lips.

I'd been waiting all my life for that kiss. After all the years of wanting it, wishing for it, fantasizing about it, I'd finally been kissed by a man. And there was more where that came from. Robert kissed me again, a little more insistently this time, playing his tongue along my upper lip. It was at that point that I asked in an understandably breathy tone if I could put the glasses down. Robert laughed and took the drinks from my hands, and put them on the counter behind me.

My hands freed, I wrapped my arms around Robert, and we kissed. Robert kissed my face and eyelids and throat, dallied his tongue tip in both my ears, making me gasp. I touched him everywhere I could reach, stroked his prickly short-short hair, kneaded big handfuls of his beige double-knit behind, and ate up Robert's sweet kisses like candy. They *were* like candy: good and plenty.

I sighed aloud as Robert unbuttoned my shirt and kissed his way down to my nipples, and sucked first one, then the other, to puckered erection. I was so full of the smell and taste and feel of this sweet hot blue-eyed man, not to mention the immediate discovery of the nipples as an erogenous zone (nobody ever told me your chest could feel quite that good), that Robert managed to have my Levi's unbuttoned and my dick out of my pants and waving him hello before I'd even noticed. Robert stepped back from me for a moment and looked at me: shirt open, pants down around my knees, leaning against my kitchen counter. He smiled a long, slow smile and said, "Beautiful."

Then he took me by the erect penis and led me (walking rather like a geisha girl, what with my pants down to my knees) to my bed.

What happened next is the stuff of the sort of story usually found between photographs of naked boys with homemade tattoos on their arms, in those dog-eared magazines you keep under the bed next to the Hot Lube, the Trojans, and that little leather whatchacallit. And this isn't one of those stories. So let's just say that, of the milestones in a young man's life − his first car, his first date, that sort of thing − few things, perhaps nothing compares with a boy's first blow job. At least, so it was for me.

It wasn't until Robert had finished, and I looked up to see him standing next to my bed, grinning that grin of his, that I realized he'd never removed a stitch of clothing. There I lay, sprawled, spent, and quite altogether naked on the bed, and there stood Robert, beige double-knit suit still very much in evidence. I was thinking of mentioning this fact when Robert said, "Hey, you."

"Hey what?" I said.

And Robert sang, softly and not quite in tune: "Happy birthday to you/Happy birthday to you/Happy birthday big Larry—"

He stopped singing, wiggled an eyebrow at me, and said, "And I *do* mean *big!*" Then he climbed back onto the bed, clothes and all, and hugged me a big, warm hug and kissed my lips, and whispered, "See you later, you little sexpot."

Then he climbed off me and off the bed, tiptoed out of the apartment, and was gone. Leaving me feeling about as good as California law will allow, touching my body where Robert had touched it, and singing softly to myself, "Happy birthday to me..."

Robert and I had sex a few times after that — once in the upstairs banquet room at McDonald's, on a table, no less. (Oh, what that man could do with mayonnaise!) But it was just fun and games — I couldn't even *pretend* to be in love with Robert, and even at eighteen I knew I wanted to be in love. So it just sort of petered out after a while. And within a year, I *was* in love. (But that's another story.)

Still, I'll never forget Robert — Larry R., that is. Or the present he gave me: my very first sexual experience — one that I'll always remember fondly. So, whether or not he ever sees the Acknowledgments to my second novel, whether he still remembers me or forgot me five minutes after our last tryst — I do hope he's well. And very happy. I honestly do.

Thomas Frasier

Coming to Terms

Every Tuesday I usually have lunch with an old friend. More often than not, we talk about our respective childhoods. While we rarely talk about sex, I was not especially surprised one Tuesday when she asked me when I first realized I was gay.

"Very early," I answered. I wasn't sure when, exactly. It seemed like I always knew it, even before I knew what "it" was.

"Did you ever feel that there was something wrong with you because you were gay?"

"No," I replied.

"You didn't feel any guilt?" she persisted.

"No."

"Really?" she asked suspiciously.

"Really," I replied, "I honestly never did."

"How wonderful!" she exclaimed.

Had my parents overlooked something while I was growing up? That seemed highly unlikely. *How,* then?

◆

I was born in a small town in the Upper Peninsula of Michigan, and raised there between the start of World War II and the end of the Korean War. If my friend at lunch was the determined survivor of a strict, upper-middle-class upbringing in a prosperous Mid-Atlantic port city, then I was equally hard pressed as a second-generation gay descendant of steerage-class immigrants, who for some inexplicable reason were attracted to one of the most remote, sparsely settled areas of the Great Lakes region.

That part of the country has a long history of absorbing immigrants, beginning with the fur traders when the area was still French. In the nineteenth century, Scandinavians and Poles came over to work in the woods, or in the iron and copper mines beside the Cornish, who arrived when the tin mines began closing in their region of England. There was also a small, clannish enclave of Greek restaurateurs, and one of Jewish merchants. Only the Finns continued to speak their native language after World War II, but even those of us who grew up speaking only English spoke it with a distinctive accent influenced by all these peoples.

The interaction of these ethnic groups was actually quite amicable, and surprisingly tolerant. In spite of some often wildly individualistic personalities, most everyone seemed reasonably flexible in forging a common life in spite of their differences. But not all differences were tolerated.

From time to time, men who lived in my hometown would leave quietly – for no apparent reason. But a lot of people were leaving. After World War II the area's economy started going downhill, and there were far more serious things for everyone to think about than their neighbor's sex life. The Upper Peninsula's biggest export was fast becoming something far more valuable than the gleanings from its war-depleted forests, or its copper and iron deposits – it was losing its people, including many gay men within the more visible exodus of straights.

45

The word *homosexual* was never used by my parents when I was growing up. When I was little, I was told not to accept candy from grown men. When I was in sixth grade, and three teenage boys gave me a ride home one day, my father said not to accept rides from them again. In both cases, no explanation was given. People didn't talk much about sex in the late '40s and early '50s, or tell someone about to enter puberty any more than absolutely necessary — unless they caught you at it!

While it's hard to keep much of anything secret in a small town, that doesn't keep very many people from doing what they want to do. One day my aunt Ann used a word I didn't know. She had been talking about Rita, a "maiden lady" who wore her prematurely gray hair cut in a boyish bob, and was a staunch member of the Methodist Church, which at the time was attracting a large following among the town's women. I don't remember now what the word was, but I do remember asking her what it meant.

Aunt Ann hesitated a moment before she answered, then she smiled and replied, "Rita likes to kiss other women the way most women like to kiss men." I had seen women kiss each other, but till then it had never occurred to me that they might kiss the same way men and women were supposed to. If two women could do that, then two men could do it, too! And that possibility excited me very much, even then — especially when I thought of some of my older sister's boyfriends.

By the time my peer group began to enter puberty, we knew all the "dirty" words. We had always known they were naughty, but now they had an entirely different meaning. And if boys got hard-ons talking dirty, that was okay. The words were *supposed* to make us bold and the girls shy. Actually, it made everyone bold — except the gays.

So what does a gay in junior high do in a small town? The same as nongays: you masturbate. And in my case, it supplied the only consummation for a secret crush I had on a quiet seventeen-year-old Finnish boy on the football team. The next year I rather impulsively joined the junior varsity football team in hopes of seeing him naked in the locker room. While I was quite smitten by my youthful idol, it did not keep me from looking at the naked bodies of the rest of the team, or from having sexual fantasies about them. After practice I used to go home and masturbate in the bathroom before dinner. Eventually, I had my first sexual encounter with a boy I'd grown up with.

One day, as I sat on the school steps with him as he waited for his mother to pick him up, he turned to me and said, "Let's fuck."

"What?" I said, not quite believing my ears.

"You heard me," he said. "We could use a good *fuck.*"

Not having done it with anyone yet, I couldn't have agreed with him more — if he meant what I thought he meant. I proceeded cautiously, "You mean, the two of us?"

"Yeah!"

"You mean, the two of us together?" I asked nervously.

"Yeah!"

"But, I mean, we're both guys...," I began lamely.

"In the ass," he cut in impatiently. "We fuck each other in the ass!"

"Okay, when?" I said before he changed his mind.

"Tomorrow morning. Your place!" he shouted over his shoulder as he ran to meet his mother, who had just driven up.

The next day was Saturday, and my folks would be out of town. It would be perfect! But he never showed up. Several weeks later, we were up in his room playing Monopoly. We were alone in the house. He repeated the suggestion, and this time we did it. I did it to him first, then he did it to me. He was letting me do it to him a second time when we heard the front door slam! We jumped up, quickly pulled on our pants, and tried to act as if nothing out of the ordinary had happened.

By the tenth grade, it had become apparent that gays had two choices: you could become a "church fairy" — which meant no sex, you went to church a lot, and one of your dad's lodge brothers would give you a desk job after you graduated. Or you could become a "barfly." In that case, you could get sex — if you didn't mind the drunks that hung out in the bars.

Of course, if you went the second route, there was always the possibility that you'd be asked to leave town. Even if you weren't, the two alternatives seemed awfully limited — even with a dozen different denominations in town, and an equal number of taverns to choose from! I saw the handwriting on the wall: I'd best leave before I found myself forced into a choice I didn't want to make.

In the meantime, I continued to have sex with the same friend I had my first encounter with, and to the best of my knowledge, we were never detected. Neither of us developed any emotional or lasting sexual interest in each other. I certainly wanted to have sex and so did he — and we both knew the other would do it. Whenever his folks were out, he'd call and ask me over to watch TV. (My family didn't have TV yet.) All I had to do was slouch down on the sofa and spread my legs, and his hand would be over on my crotch. Then he'd unzip my pants, reach in, pull out my cock, and play with it while we watched the tube! Just when I'd think I couldn't hold back any longer, he would offer to let me fuck him, which I did. Sometimes we went up to his room; other times we got so hot we did it right there on the sofa.

This went on for about a year, then he started talking about girls. I wasn't about to go out looking for girls with him, so I suggested he fuck me. When he didn't seem very enthusiastic, I told him to close his eyes and pretend he was doing it to a girl. He did, but then he wanted to kiss, and I didn't. Not with him, anyway.

In the meantime, I was becoming more interested in doing it with other guys, but I was afraid of the rumors that would start about me. It was simply easier — and far less risky — for the two of us to keep on doing it with each other. His interest in having sex with me may have waned, but not his interest in having sex. Girls who would mess around could get any guy they wanted. And they had a definite preference for guys on the football or basketball team, which my friend definitely was not. While he never made the first move again, he never refused to go along when I did.

He may have thought about girls while we were doing it, but I knew I had absolutely no interest in trying it with one, and carefully avoided any situation where I might be forced into it. Fortunately, my parents never asked me why I didn't have a girlfriend, which took a lot of pressure off me. Still, it was a no-win situation. I didn't want to become the town whore, but I wasn't interested in becoming its newest saint, either. My parents would have preferred me to be straight, but they would settle for saint — if that meant we wouldn't have to talk about it. We never did talk about it then — not ever, really. But as I said, I left as soon as I could. My folks wanted me to go to college, and I jumped at the chance.

Once, when I was home on break, I began asking my father about which friends were still around and what they were doing. I casually mentioned Jerry Kennedy. Jerry had graduated ahead of me, and I had heard things about him. My father looked uncomfortable, and wondered why I should ask.

"Oh, no special reason," I replied breezily.

Jerry had been on the football and basketball teams. I figured it was safe to mention him. Everyone knew him. Sullen, arrogant, he positively oozed sexuality.

"He's at Newberry," my father replied. Newberry was the state mental hospital. "Got to drinking, and pesterin' other guys. His folks had him committed."

I never mentioned his name again; there was no doubt what my dad had meant by "pesterin'." But Jerry had been so hot-looking – the way he would strut around, his chunky little Irish ass bouncing insolently – and one of the few guys in the tenth grade who had enough facial hair to grow an honest-to-goodness moustache! And those black, flashing eyes...

That semester, I fell hopelessly in love with someone in my dormitory. Not only did I want to have sex with him, I wanted to make love to him. But nothing happened. Then during spring semester finals, he asked if I would be his roommate next year, and I said yes. As it turned out, he reciprocated my feelings and we did make love together. Although he was reluctant to do more than indulge in a few furtive, guilt-ridden encounters, I was in heaven. I had found what I knew I had been instinctively looking for. It was not so simple for my roommate. He flunked out at the end of the year and, rather than face his family, ran off and joined the army. I was devastated.

My last year in college, I knew I would have to tell my parents that I did not want to return home after graduation, but I dreaded it. Could I get away with not telling the real reason? If I went back, could I really live at home again? What about sex? Would they kick me out if I was sexually active? Even if they didn't, what about the town?

The questions remained unanswered. Actually, they never got asked. I got a job right after college with a company that moved me around to several midwestern cities. My first impression of gay life in these cities — in the early '60s — was relief! There *was* a place for people like me after all. I quickly learned I could do pretty much what I wanted. City neighbors had almost no interest, and even less control, over whom you went to bed with.

That isn't all I learned. I remember walking down the street with a friend one Sunday afternoon in Indianapolis. We were on our way to a party when a young man leaned out the window of a passing car and let out a line of expletives ending in "fucking queers." Frankly, I didn't realize he was yelling at us. Not so my city-bred friend. He yelled right back, shaking his fist after the car.

Later, at the party, everyone thought it a very bold and foolhardy thing for him to do. I think a lot of gay people who grow up in small towns and rural areas are dumbfounded by the open hostility they find in the cities directed at gays. It wasn't like that back home for most of us. But was it because they accepted it? Or because we were still unsure of our sexuality when we left?

◆

As I walked back to my office after lunch with my friend, I thought about my aunt's remark, and the woman who liked to kiss women. Rita was always cheerful and hearty. Especially compared with so many of the women in my hometown, saddled with children, with insensitive or abusive husbands, clothes to wash, and endless meals to cook. And there was something about this slim-hipped, big-bosomed woman that they responded to instinctively. Rita was not unfriendly to men, but her eyes would positively light up when one of these women said hello to her. She simply loved them for themselves.

As I sat down at my desk, I suddenly realized how much I envied Rita's rapport with these women. There was no man in my hometown even remotely her male counterpart. Undoubtedly some of that was because Rita was simply Rita, a wonderfully free soul, but she was also a woman. A man in the '50s wasn't allowed to feel about another man the way Rita felt about women.

Back then, the older men I met in gay bars seemed shockingly frivolous in comparison to someone like Rita. They were not warm and loving — they were absolutely obsessed with being found out and losing their jobs. They spent a lot of money sending drinks to young hunks they were afraid would otherwise have nothing to do with them, which was generally true enough. It was not so much that they were silly old men spending too much money, but they seemed to be so compromised by life. They made the men my age very uncomfortable — because if something didn't change, someday that would be our fate, too.

The Stonewall riots of 1969, thank God, changed all that. Still, it's not enough that construction workers wear their hair longer than most drag queens would have dared in the '50s! I wanted someone who would be more than a father, or a brother, or even a fuck buddy. I grew up longing for the company of another male, someone who would have been allowed the same latitude women like Rita were given. Someone who could touch me, and teach me about myself. Today this seems even less likely than it did thirty-five years ago, considering what we now know about child abuse. Interaction between grown men and other, younger males is now more suspect than ever. Even if it were possible to isolate the sexual component from the rest of a young boy's needs and put it on hold, how can one possibly hope to allay the fears of a society where men are routinely abusive?

It's still a far from perfect world, but at least no one need spend life on the sidelines just because they are gay. Even if you're not especially good at asserting yourself, you don't have to settle for living an incomplete life. There *is* a gay world out there. And the rest of the world knows it!

Even though it's simply easier to be gay in a big city, there's something to be said for growing up gay in a small town, at least as I remember it in the '50s. Maybe I was just lucky. I had a father who believed in the equality of all people, and argued it with all the passion men in his generation brought to their convictions, and my aunt Ann, who had the courage to tell a shy young boy the simple truth. Jerry Kennedy, who grew up only a few blocks from me, was not so lucky.

Growing up is a fearful business in any time or place. It's a wonder that anyone gets through it. But we survive. And when it comes time to make the important decisions in our lives — like coming to terms with our sexuality — all we need do is look to the example of the few, very special people who touched our lives. And then we can set aside childhood fears, take a deep breath, and get on with life.

Vernon Maulsby

Nightwings

I grew up in the '60s, between acid rock and rock and roll. Just before I entered my teens, I had my first crush and lover. His name was Eddie, a slim, dark-eyed boy, perhaps a year younger than I was. We had always been inseparable as children; we seemed a natural team, and our families gave no notice. No one thought it odd that we preferred each other's company over other people's. We were known and accepted as loners, plus neither one of us was popular in or out of school — me 'cause of my obesity and color, Eddie 'cause of his habitually long silences when all he wanted to do was think about things or write his poetry.

In 1969 we became lovers. It wasn't planned or expected — it just happened one day while we were stretched out together on the couch watching TV. His parents had just told him about their upcoming divorce and custody fight. Neither parent wanted him and made it evident. He cried in my arms; I felt angry and wanted to protect him, shield him from the pain. I had butterflies in my stomach and felt feverish. He looked up while I held him and kissed me. We slowly, fumblingly made love, and I felt complete for the first time in my life. Nothing had ever felt so right before. We cleaned up in the shower and went back to watching TV.

We never made love again. What came naturally to me was "wrong" to Eddie. Our friendship was soon on the skids, and we consciously avoided each other. The word *homosexual,* or the thought of being gay, never entered my mind. I was just me, and I thought Eddie was a once-in-a-lifetime love.

Sex, of any kind, was a forbidden subject in my home. All I ever remember hearing was that when the "right" person came along I would know it. I know they meant a woman, but to my family that was an obvious fact that didn't need mentioning. In my highly religious home, lots of things were taken for granted, with no effort made to spell them out. As a member of the only black family in an upper-middle-class suburb in upstate New York, there was a certain distance between me and normal social interaction. Being the minister's grandson, and fat too, I was really on my own, even as far as my moral precepts went. Eddie felt right, and that was enough.

In my early teens, I had my first experience with females. I was capable physically, but something was missing. I thought that was just how straight sex was supposed to be, so I accepted my lack of enthusiasm as normal.

I was always one of those kids who wandered around town, just killing time – especially after Eddie and I broke up. One evening I was sitting on the pier, watching the Hudson River go by, when I met my first gay person. He was a cute guy in his thirties, just wandering around like me. We spoke for a while, and I started feeling butterflies, like before. We stopped talking and just looked at each other. I was scared and happy at the same time as I took him home. My mom was out, so it was safe, and I wanted this man in my bed so bad my teeth itched. Later I learned his name was Terri; he was the guy that they had talked about in town as being "queer." I began to panic. What if someone had seen us together? He understood and left his phone number in case I wanted to meet him again.

We snuck around together for a couple of years. He cared enough about me to put up with my crap without complaints. He just lived as an example of how it could be and was patient with me. In 1973, he told me he was in love with me and wanted me to either move in, or at least admit that I was gay and stop hiding.

So, as far as my social life went, I came out. Terri helped me find my space. His advice was always available. He let me try my wings and was always there when I landed hard. He understood about my continued hiding from my parents and didn't press me — he said it would come with time and that I'd know when I was ready.

Until he moved in 1975, we were a couple. I didn't go with him, because as I had grown, I learned that my needs had changed. We remained close friends until his death in 1982.

I went through a rough time about his death; he died by his own hand. We had spoken by phone the week before it happened, and, as far as I could tell, he was okay. He just came home from work and cut his wrists in the bathtub.

The services were closed to me once the family heard my name, but I made it to the graveside and paid my respects. I managed to put my bracelet in the grave so that something of me could be with him. That may sound silly, but it felt right.

After I graduated from high school, I moved into my own apartment and began college. I worked in a hospital, and there I met my lover Percy. When I first saw him, it was no big thing, but in the next few days I stopped in to check on his recovery. I knew he was gay the second time I talked to him, but things didn't gel until, as I was leaving one day, he threw his shorts at my head and walked naked into his bathroom. I'm lucky he had a private room, because we didn't wait.

When he got released, I left work early to take him home.

When Percy and I made plans to live together, I knew it was time to be honest with my mom. I made a big thing of it, rehearsing for weeks in front of my mirror while shaving, in the car on the way to school, and so on. I made reservations at this nice restaurant for us; I wanted everything just right.

Things went completely wrong. I ended up telling her over tea that afternoon. I just looked into her eyes and told her. My prepared speech (with historical footnotes) went right out the window. As I talked with my mother and told her I was gay and had been for as long as I could remember, she just sat there sipping her tea. She took her glasses off, smiled, and told me she had known for years. After my jaw closed I started to cry; I couldn't help it. The pressure was off, and I couldn't stop. She held me tight, and we had a good cry together. I didn't lose her love as I had feared: she didn't like my choice, but she supported me. We became closer as the years passed.

The rest of the family ostracized me. I was no longer welcome in their homes or around their children. They feared that my gayness was contagious. My cousins were told that I was "sick" and they should stay away from me. It hurt, but Mom and Percy helped me get through it. Since my mother's death in 1982, my family and I live our own lives. Our contacts are few and far between.

My growth as a black gay person has been gradual, nurtured by both straight and gay people who loved me for who I am. Today I am free to live and love as I choose because of their support.

> I have my wings
> and Now
> I can Fly.

Bert Wylen

Out of Hell's Fire,
Into the Frying Pan

I came out of the closet as the result of some powerful spiritual experiences. I had grown up steeped in Jewish studies and traditions, and although I declared myself an atheist at age nineteen, I look back on that "conversion" today as just another part of my relationship with God. Today, I know in my heart, in my soul, and in my mind that God made me homosexual, that in fact God who is all things *is* homosexual, and that my activism for gay and lesbian causes fulfills my ministry for God.

I became an atheist as the result of my first philosophy course at Temple University. I had been struggling for a number of years with my concepts of God, the universe, infinity — ideas that, one hopes, one gives up trying to reckon before the brain twists itself into a knot. The professor of the course one day explained that he was an atheist because he could find no proof of God's existence. He said he believed that anybody who chose to believe in any kind of god was possessed of a spiritual vacuum that they were too weak-minded or lazy to fill themselves.

That sounded good to me. It was simple, direct, and freed me from all my troubled thoughts. I declared myself an atheist and let the universe worry about itself for a while.

Some time later, I was studying the works of John Milton in an English course. Anyone who knows anything about Milton knows that you've got to study the New Testament in order to extract the intended meaning from his work. I had never read the New Testament, as it was forbidden reading in my family. Having read the Gospel according to Matthew, I couldn't understand why I had been deprived of its teachings. This man Jesus was full of good sense, good conscience, and great love — all the qualities that we "counterculture" types had tried to personify.

Jesus said, "Ask and you shall receive, seek and you shall find, knock and the door shall be opened to you." So I asked, "Okay, Jesus, if you're really there, I'd like to know you, so come on in!" Not long after that, I had an immensely powerful spiritual experience, where I felt myself transported from my chair in the living room and into the presence of God. The cynic would call it an out-of-body experience. So be it. Who am I to argue? For me, however, the experience launched a spiritual journey that continues to this day.

I sought out the Holy Spirit. I came to rely upon the Bible for guidance and inspiration on a daily basis. God satisfied my every need. I felt truly joyful for the first time in my life. My inquisitiveness grew stronger every day, and my hunger for righteousness was filled.

God even spoke to me, not in the same buddy-buddy way he apparently talks to Oral Roberts, but more intimately, in a manner that I came to trust. When I was at a loss for an answer, for an inspiration, I could simply open my Bible and the passage I needed would leap out at me from the page (I've heard this called Bible Roulette). God also spoke to me, and continues to do so, through the people around me. Somehow

I always get what I need, though not always what I want when I want it.

A Bible verse promises the heavenly benevolence that I experienced (metaphorically, of course) at that point in my awakening:

> It shall come to pass, if you shall hearken diligently unto My commandments which I command you this day, to love the Lord your God, and to serve with all your heart, and with all your soul, that I will give the rain of your land in its season, the former rain and the latter rain, that you may gather in your corn, and your wine, and your oil. And I will give grass in your fields for your cattle, and you shall eat and be satisfied. (Deuteronomy 11:13–15)

All this time, though I was for the most part happy and enjoying my spiritual growth, my sexuality caused me problems: emotional suffering and spiritual anguish. I had internalized every homo-hating concept heaped on me by society. In no way, however, was I seeking a spiritual awakening because I thought that that might *cure* me of homosexuality. In fact, I thought that all I needed was to find the right girl, and all those lustful thoughts and feelings aroused by hot boys would just vanish.

Meanwhile, that summer, armed with my Bible, a backpack full of clothes, and a sleeping bag, I hitchhiked across the Catskill Mountains of New York, seeking to strengthen my personal relationship with Jesus Christ. I hitchhiked through little mountain hamlets, with nothing but lonely desolation and an occasional car in between them. My only sense of security came from the green mountains that rose up around me and a hunting knife clipped to my belt, which I quickly lost.

Every driver that picked me up on that journey spoke to me about the Lord, with no prompting from me. Having done a lot of hitchhiking in my day, this really shocked me, because it had never happened to me. Here I was, calling upon God to reveal himself, and he did through my communion with my fellow travelers. I felt the presence of God in those moments more intensely than I have felt it since, perhaps because I found it so new, so exciting, so wondrous.

Finally, after about five days in the mountains, I was born again. This guy picked me up on Interstate 81 going south out of Binghamton, New York. He was pulling a trailer full of wood-burning stoves from upstate to Reading, Pennsylvania, behind a jeep that had lost its muffler. When he started speaking about the Lord, I told him the purpose of my spiritual journey, and that I was hoping to be born again into the Holy Spirit. With a whole bunch of "Praise God's," "Thank the Good Lord's," and "Oh, Jesus Christ's," I was born again right there in the jeep, declaring my salvation at the top of my lungs so we both could hear it above the roar of the unmuffled engine. I felt uneasy when the guy told me that it would be better if I held his hand while I made my declaration, I guess for fellowship, and I remember thinking, "Oh God! He's a fag!" Just my internalized homo-hatred haunting me.

Now, while I hadn't been seeking the Lord in order to cure my homosexuality, I found that, more than ever before, a feeling of shame and self-loathing swept over me every time I felt an attraction for, or had a sexual fantasy about, another man. I felt corrupt; that these feelings were not right in the eyes of God, and therefore were preventing me from being filled with righteousness.

About half a year after my born-again experience, at age twenty-four, I had sex for the first time with another guy. He was gorgeous, an all-around athlete, and, what's more, he inspired me in ways I had never dreamed of. He aroused feelings of love that I'd never felt, and thought I'd never feel. To have sex, we had to be drunk, and each time was our "last time before going back to women." We had our last time about four or five times a week for around two and a half years. The relationship was sick. We finally broke apart, and haven't spoken since. But I loved him as I loved no other, and may never love again.

I went a few months after our breakup without sex, and then I couldn't take it anymore. I knew about gay bars, but, because I was filled with the self-importance that comes with having a big-moneyed career, I didn't want to risk being seen around a gay bar — especially since I still wasn't sure whether or not I was really gay. Denial is an awesome thing. So I went into the city, picked up a copy of the *Philadelphia Gay News,* and looked for an "escort," thinking that, if I wasn't really gay and my affair with the love of my life was a fluke, then I wouldn't get turned on by another guy.

I got turned on.

That was a pivotal point in my coming out. In a moment of sanity, I realized that I could no longer deny my sexuality. I knew I was homosexual. I determined to find out exactly what that meant.

My opportunity came later that year when the computer company I worked for promoted me to New England regional sales manager and I moved to Waterbury, Connecticut. I figured I could explore the gay "lifestyle" away from family, friends, and the risk of exposure. I thought I'd just test it out, have some great sex, and then return to my closet forever.

I moved to New England on January 1, 1984. Almost immediately, I looked up the word *gay* in the phone book and found a listing for the gay switchboard in New Haven. I dialed.

When someone answered, I hung up, too scared and too ashamed to speak to a "homosexual." I continued to do that for nearly three months, until the loneliness just got too much for me. I hung in there one evening and spoke to the man who answered the phone.

I asked for directions to the gay bars, never thinking for a moment that homosexuals did anything but go to bars to pick each other up for sex. He obliged me, but as I was ready to hang up he managed to tell me about a congregation of gay and lesbian Christians. They met in a church on the Yale campus in New Haven on Sunday afternoons, and I was welcome to worship with them. How unusual, I thought, that a bunch of godless homosexuals would form a church. My curiosity stimulated, I took the 45-minute drive that Sunday. That's how I found the Metropolitan Community Church.

A bundle of raw nerves, I sweated out every mile in fear. Would they think I was one of them? Would going lock me into some sort of commitment to their "lifestyle"? Would they try to have sex with me? What if someone saw me going in?

To make matters worse, I arrived to find that Yale was celebrating Spring Fling. People were everywhere. I found the church, but every time I tried to open the door, I chickened out and walked away. I tried so hard to convince myself that I wasn't really gay. But God must have known what he was doing when he sent me there during Spring Fling. Every time I had convinced myself that I could "straighten out," I saw another gorgeous shirtless sweaty college boy flinging a Frisbee or jumping and stretching for a volleyball, and I was reminded of the truth.

After about forty-five minutes of false starts, I finally opened the church door. I stayed for the entire service, being careful not to make eye contact with anybody for too long, and sitting at the back of the room. How I wished they had a curtain for me to hide behind. Afterward, they served coffee, and I managed to stay for a few minutes. I'll never forget the kindheartedness of those people — they seemed to sense my fear and anguish, and they were exceedingly gentle with me. They made me feel welcome, unintimidated, and willing to accept their invitation to come back every week.

After a month or two of Sundays, I accepted the pastor's invitation to set an appointment to talk with him. Jim Burns was a 24- or 25-year-old divinity student at Yale, and was ministering to MCC until a full-time pastor could be located. I arrived at Jim's office one weekday evening, coming from work dressed up in my IBM-type drag.

After a minimal amount of small talk, Jim got right to the point. "Why did you want to speak with me?" he asked.

I wasn't really prepared to divulge that at that moment, so I beat nervously around the bush. "I need help with my 'problem,'" I replied.

"What problem is that?" Jim asked.

"Well, you know, my problem with my sexuality."

"What problem with your sexuality?"

I remember thinking, "You bastard!" He was going to force me to say it out loud, to hear myself with my own words come right out and admit, "I'm a homosexual." I said it barely audibly, and with a lot of stumbling on the *h* word. It was finally out. To hear myself say it took a great heaviness off of my psyche.

Jim smiled. "There now, that wasn't so bad, was it?"

Finally, I had found a group of God-loving people where I fit in, who wouldn't judge me, throw the Bible at me, and treat me as an outsider. I was one of them. I could now own that. I made an agreement with Jim to attend church every Sunday, to participate in an evening Bible study every Wednesday, and to help support the church financially.

I thrived at MCC. I grew in acceptance of my sexuality, and even became willing to be seen in public with my new gay and lesbian friends. In the beginning, my fellow MCCers were always trying to get me to go out for a drink or a bite to eat after church on Sundays, but I continually refused, afraid that they'd "act gay" and we'd all be harassed and possibly beaten up. I went out a few times, but I always felt like a little fish that had spent its life in a ten-gallon tank. Suddenly, I had been poured out into a vast ocean.

Nine months later, I was back in Philadelphia, having left the employ of the company that had sent me to Connecticut. Leaving the comfortable nest that my MCC friends had made for me, I wasn't able to bring myself to hook up with MCC in Philly. I spent my thirty-first birthday, a bitter cold night in January, with my godchild's parents, who have since stopped speaking to me because of my sexuality. When I left them, I went to a gay bar. I sat there getting drunk, tormented by shame, and fearful that someone would find out that I was queer.

A few days later I chanced upon Pat Robertson's *700 Club* on television, which was holding a telethon. For some reason, I left it on. Robertson announced that "a homosexual in Michigan has accepted Jesus Christ, forsaken his sinful lifestyle, and has pledged a hundred dollars." I decided that, relying upon my relationship with Jesus, I too would stop being homosexual. Thank God, I didn't send that criminal any money.

Forsaking all the heavenly direction I had gotten about my sexuality, forgetting all the wonderful gay and lesbian Christians who had shared their warmth and their love with me, I "went straight."

And the second half of God's promise quoted earlier came true for me:

> Take heed to yourselves, lest your heart be deceived, and you turn aside, and serve other gods, and worship them; and the displeasure of the Lord will be aroused against you, and God will shut up the heaven, so that there shall be no rain, and the ground shall not yield her fruit; and you'll perish quickly from off the good land which the Lord has given you. (Deuteronomy 11:16–17)

I was, in fact, now serving gods other than my own Creator, and they had names like Robertson, Falwell, and Kennedy. The displeasure of my Lord with my life was apparent. I stopped producing revenues for my new company, and therefore income for myself. I became increasingly depressed, and I drank and drugged myself into a stupor every night. I couldn't sleep at night, couldn't get out of bed in the morning, and didn't function all day. God had shut up the heaven in which I had thrived.

The worst thing was that God had stopped talking to me. I enjoyed no fellowship with other Christians, only the shame and self-loathing that came with listening to those "other gods." And when I opened my Bible, it no longer spoke to me.

One night in May of 1985, I was suffering pitiful and incomprehensible demoralization. I could take it no more. I got down on my knees at the dining room table, and prayed that God would deliver me. "Tell me what you want from me, and I will do it. Just take my miserable life from me," I pleaded.

I sat at the table, and, as it happened, I opened the Bible to the first page of the book of Jonah. That discouraged me, because I thought it was just a children's tale about a man and a whale. I read it anyway.

Jonah was a man of God, a messenger of the Almighty, charged with going to the city of Nineveh to proclaim God's anger against the people there. But Jonah was afraid and rebelled against God, booking passage on a ship going to Tarshish instead. A great storm threatened the ship on its journey and was near destruction when Jonah, knowing that God's anger was upon him, told the ship's crew to throw him overboard. Jonah was swallowed up into the belly of a great fish, where he stayed three days and three nights. He repented his disobedience to God, and God forgave Jonah. The fish vomited Jonah up on dry land, and Jonah fulfilled his ministry to Nineveh.

I knew, sitting there in my gloom, that God had just spoken to me, for the first time since I had rebuked him and decided to go back in the closet.

God had given me talents and abilities to develop: a knack for organizing, for motivating and counseling people, for writing, and for fighting long battles. All my life I had used these abilities: in the civil rights movement of the '60s and '70s; in the protests and marches against the Vietnam War, as well as for Soviet Jewry; in my college fraternity, even occasionally on the editorial page of the local newspaper. My greatest fear about being gay, the one that made me most like Jonah, was that God expected me to use these talents for the gay cause, and not to bury them in the ground. Like Jonah, I had tried to run away.

Right there I tried to make a deal with God. I said, "Okay, I understand that you're telling me you created me homosexual, and that you've got work for me to do. But please, let me stay in some sort of closet, not too open, but just open enough that I can grab a cute young lover and live happily ever after in wedded bliss."

That was not God's will for me. A week later, I was sitting in the office of a therapist whom I had found through the

Philadelphia Gay News, to help me find my way out of the closet. I made weekly visits to Giovanni's Room, the local gay bookstore, and I read voraciously about gay life and the gay community. A year later, I was writing for the gay press.

Today, I host and produce a popular weekly radio program called *Gaydreams,* and I produce features for another weekly program, *This Way Out: The International Lesbian and Gay Radio Magazine.* Because of my willingness to be outspoken on gay issues and because of rampant homophobia in the world of journalism, I have not always been able to secure sufficient monetary compensation to keep a roof over my head. I ended up homeless for about a year. Although I was destitute, I managed to continue producing gay radio (I call it being "radio-active") and even some television, managing to get some of my productions into the mainstream media.

I consider what I do today to be my ministry for God, helping people to learn to love themselves and win their own battles with homo-hatred. I look at my hardships as opportunities for spiritual growth. If God wanted me doing something else, then other opportunities would present themselves to me. When circumstances seem as though they'll finally break me and I get it in my mind to quit, I always get another letter from some gay teenager telling me that hearing my program saved his or her life. So many gay and lesbian kids think they're alone, and through the singularly personal medium of radio, now they know they're not.

Jesus said that you can tell whether a tree is good or bad by the fruit it produces. All fruit jokes aside, I can see by the impact of my "radio ministry" that this tree produces good fruit. Many people partake of it and are made whole in the acceptance of their sexuality. Each week I close my show with the creed that I hope to pass on to my listeners: Be happy, be safe, and be gay!

M.A. Williams

Out of the Cocoon

When I was a kid, the word *gay* could always get a few giggles whenever my class would stumble upon it in a story or poem we happened to be studying. Of course, our teacher would always remind us of its older definition of "happiness," but being happy didn't seem to have anything to do with the meaning we had in mind.

Looking back, I see how we were victims of our parents' ignorance. To them the word *gay* stood for everything they didn't want in a son or daughter. The Church taught that homosexuality was unnatural and immoral, and my parents supported that view, because they didn't know what being gay really meant. I grew up fearing the word, just as I did any other dirty word that threatened a mouth full of soap.

However, I now find that the word that would have insulted me at one time now makes me proud. Such new meaning comes in the realization of the fact that *gay* is a word that describes me, and it is my hope that in my life, homosexuality and happiness will not be totally unrelated, but will complement one another and lead people to a better understanding of me and others like me.

The realization of my homosexuality was a gradual one. As I ended seventh grade at the age of thirteen, puberty introduced me to the awakening of my sexual desires. As I became more aware of the pleasures that could come from sex, I began to find that my preferences were for other guys. I did not have any sexual relations with anyone, but I found that in masturbating, my fantasies centered on other guys and not on girls.

Although by the eighth grade I felt I had established my sexual preference, I still hadn't really accepted the idea that I was gay. I just didn't feel comfortable with the label, especially because of all the negative connotations it held for me at the time.

In junior high I was very shy and reserved. I had a low sense of self-esteem, because I didn't see myself as popular or good-looking, and I couldn't see why anyone would want me as a friend. I didn't need another reason to look down on myself.

But in high school, my self-image gradually began to change. I began to come out of the shell I had built for protection, and I began to believe that some people might actually find me attractive as a friend. I became more open and outgoing, and found that when I was friendly to people, they didn't reject me.

While this enriched my life and gave me a heightened sense of self-worth, I still lacked the hope that any of my friends would accept the idea that I was gay. Inside, I continued to struggle to suppress my homosexuality, which conflicted with my desire to be honest with others. I became depressed that I had no one I could really open up to and who would be understanding and accepting. I don't know how I ever would have pulled myself out of such depths of despair if it were not for the Alyson Letter Exchange Program.

Until I discovered it, everything seemed hopeless, but I'll never forget the night I accidentally stumbled upon a radio talk show that just happened to be discussing homosexuality. I listened in awe to an actual discussion of this taboo subject on the air, and frantically scribbled down the address of the pen pal service that they gave as a resource for young homosexuals who needed to open up to someone.

I immediately took their suggestion and obtained a P.O. box; then I sent off my first letter to the service. With it went all my elated hopes for contacting the person who could become the true friend that I had always wanted.

Unfortunately, my first correspondents didn't work out, but I was not about to let my hopes be dashed so soon, and I wrote off for another pen pal.

This time, my prayers were answered. I began a correspondence with Ken, from Michigan, who has since become one of my closest friends. He has given me all the understanding and acceptance that I could have ever hoped for.

We began writing in December 1985, when I was sixteen and he was almost eighteen. He had just come out to his parents, and they accepted him, a fact I found encouraging.

Over the next few months, he began to come out to some of his closer friends, and he found that those people who were his true friends still liked him and accepted his homosexuality as merely another facet of his personality. They were even glad that he had allowed them to understand him better by sharing this part of himself that they had not known before. This brightened my hope of someday finding friends who would accept my homosexuality, but I still wasn't quite ready to open up to any of my friends.

In the meantime, I came in contact with another guy through the letter exchange, but the relationship that developed between us became more than just a friendship.

His name was Michael, and he was a sophomore at a large, distant university in Iowa. From the first letter, I felt an attraction for him that was unlike any I had felt for another guy. He seemed to be everything I could have dreamed of in a lover. He was intelligent, very talented, and even handsome, and I was elated to find that he had an equally strong attraction for me.

I was overcome by the desire to meet him in person, and it was with great anticipation that I enrolled in a two-week summer music camp at the college he attended.

I couldn't believe I had really done it! I mean, there I was, someone who had once believed himself to be totally incapable of being loved, now preparing to meet someone who could become his first lover!

I was very nervous, and thoroughly horrified that he might not like me at all upon seeing me in the flesh. My fears were put to rest when we met, for he expressed the deepest and sincerest friendship for me, something for which I was even less prepared than I was for rejection.

Even though I had made some good friends in high school, I had never known anyone who had a romantic interest in me. I guess I had lots of self-doubts about ever becoming involved in such a relationship, but as Michael and I spent more time together, I found our relationship leaning more and more toward a romantic one.

This was something that I had a lot of trouble accepting. I had developed such a strong fear of being rejected by anyone I cared a lot about that whenever I felt myself getting close to them, I would try to detach myself and hide my true feelings from them. I believed that if I didn't let people know I liked them a lot, I couldn't be disappointed by finding out that they didn't feel the same way about me.

But as Michael's love for me became more and more apparent, I began to realize what harm I was really causing both of us by being too afraid to show the love that I did indeed feel for him.

Gradually, I allowed myself to open up to him. I cannot fully put into words the great joy and happiness that I felt in the sharing of our mutual love for one another. It was the most tremendous feeling I had ever encountered in my life, and it is one I will never forget. Unfortunately, that feeling did not last long.

From the beginning, we had both been aware of our limited time together, but neither of us would admit that my last day at camp was fast approaching. When it did come, I expected a painful good-bye, but I had hoped that we could continue to write until the next time we could meet.

That didn't happen. On our last day together, Michael told me that he had decided he couldn't be gay for the rest of his life. The whole time we had been together, we had felt the pressure to be secretive about our relationship, which had put a lot of strain on our love for one another. This was a strain that Michael could not put up with. He felt that he could never really have a successful long-term relationship with another guy, and so he said he would rather look for finite relationships during college, and that he would eventually settle down and get married to a girl, like "everybody else."

What surprised me more than this was how calmly I accepted the situation. I knew that we had been put under some unnecessary stress by our attempt to keep our love hidden, but I believed that in the future we would have gradually found ourselves more comfortable in showing our love for one another, regardless of those around us. I wish he had given us a chance. I thought it would have been worth the wait.

My time with Michael has become a treasured memory. For even though our relationship failed, I was successful in overcoming my own insecurities and allowing myself to love and to be loved.

That in itself is a greater joy than many people allow themselves in their entire lives, and I believe that I have just begun to live. At times, I do become depressed when I think about how difficult it is to make a gay relationship succeed, but I still have hope, and that's one word that will always serve as a promise that with the future will come change for the better.

John J. Carr

Closets Are Not for Living In

A gay senior's story

The term *coming out,* as it is presently used in our community, would have meant nothing to most of my generation when we were young. There are now almost as many meanings to the term as there are gay people. Since breaking through these painful barriers fairly late in my life, I have found that coming out is not necessarily a one-time process, and that it contains great potential for individual growth, limited only by an individual's willingness to participate.

As a community, we have developed a variety of support systems which have been generated by our own needs as gays and lesbians. Two of these support systems have made the difference for me. The first, the gay group of Alcoholics Anonymous, helped me to get back in control of my life. They not only showed me the way to a life free of alcohol, but also validated me as a gay person. The second was Dignity, an association of lesbian and gay Roman Catholics, which enhanced this process by teaching me, in a way that was not based on an archaic theology, that gay people had a spiritual side to their beings which could be developed in accordance with their needs. I will always be profoundly grateful to both groups, as well as to many in the larger gay community who have played an important role in my own self-acceptance.

◆

I was born in Chicago in August 1920 and all but grew up inside the doors of the beautiful Servite Church of Our Lady of Sorrows on Chicago's West Side, where my parents had been married. When I graduated from a Catholic grammar school, I immediately entered the preparatory novitiate of a monastic order, where I remained for three years. I cannot conceive of any way in which my upbringing could have been more strongly influenced by the proscriptive doctrines of Roman Catholicism. My mother passed away when I was ten years old, and, along with my younger sister, I was given over to the care of my father's aunt, already seventy years old. She died when I was sixteen. My relationship with my father, never a quality one, went into a steady decline from which it never fully recovered.

During those years I unconsciously internalized homophobia along with the rest of society, and this became one of my survival techniques. The economic climate created by the Great Depression, among other things, put the possibilities of higher education beyond my reach. As my father had never provided for me in any meaningful way, and since I left the Carmelite Order on my great aunt's passing, I became acutely aware that there were no options open to me except to join the work force. I found a job on the railroad.

Shortly after Pearl Harbor, I enlisted in the navy at the age of twenty-one. I was sent to the Naval Training Station at San Diego for indoctrination and training. Shortly after getting out of boot camp I sought out the Roman Catholic chaplain to try to reconcile my erotic attraction to other men with what I had been taught by the Church. My experience with Roman Catholic clergy up to that time had provided me with a sense of assurance that what I was relating to a priest, in or out of the confessional, was being treated as confidential. My "confidential" disclosures to the chaplain became the basis for my separation from the service. The armed forces could not tolerate queers. We were not even accorded the privilege of confidentiality with our own clergy!

I received an honorable discharge, but this was small consolation. My trust had been violated by someone I had been brought up to believe could be trusted. I was hurt and confused. After being discharged in San Diego, I returned to Chicago, lonelier than I have ever been at any time during my life. Money was not a problem, at least in the short term. I had enough to keep me going until I went back to work. I had been on military leave from the railroad, and I was assured by law of reinstatement. What I needed most I did not have: someone I could trust and to whom I could reach out in this time of emotional need. Life was not simplified by the fact that I was now in the minority of 22-year-olds who were not in military uniforms during wartime. One small ray of sunshine in all of this was that my Selective Service classification reverted to 1-C, which indicated that I had served honorably and had been discharged, rather than 4-F, the classification of those who were totally rejected for whatever reasons.

I returned to work for the railroad company by which I had been employed prior to entering military service. During this time, in the early 1940s, I learned about an area at the Illinois Central Railroad Station in Chicago which today we would call a "cruising" area. Even though I was doing nothing illegal, my continuing presence there provided an opportunity for a criminal, who identified himself as a plainclothes policeman, to prey on my fear by frightening me into showing him my railroad I.D., along with a savings passbook on a Chicago bank. Armed with the knowledge that I had a small amount of money in one of the banks, this individual made thinly veiled "suggestions" that there might be a way to keep my employer from finding out. It is not beyond the realm of possibility that this person was in fact a member of the Chicago Police Department. The fact is that I had been victimized by a blackmailer to the tune of about three hundred dollars, a considerable sum in those days. It was all I had, but I was too terrified to try to do anything about it, if indeed the authorities would have done anything anyway. I was not the type of citizen who warranted assistance.

The experience with the blackmailer terrified me more than I realized at the time, and this unpleasant memory only served to increase my paranoia and fear of being discovered by "Big Brother" or some other ghostly disciplinary authority. For these reasons I chose the relative safety and security of ano-nymity over the risks of exposure and the calamities that would follow if I had tried to identify myself in any way. I was fearful of going into the bars which were the center of what social life there was for us. Consequently, I never had the opportunity, in any realistic sense, of becoming part of what-ever social groups there may have been. The forerunner of today's gay bars, known as "queer joints," were few and far between, and the ones which did survive usually were in back alleys or other unsavory locations in the larger cities. Even then, a patron's peace of mind in such a place was usually in direct proportion to the "insurance" payments made by the bar's proprietor to the police department. Police raids on queer joints were not uncommon, with the patrons herded into the Black Maria and off to the slammer, and often to exposure, loss of employment, loss of reputation, and sometimes to ultimate breakdown and suicide. This at least was one indignity which I was spared, but for the remainder of my stay in the Midwest, I burrowed ever more deeply into my subterranean cave, keeping my true identity hidden and trying to make the best of a bad bargain.

In 1945 I decided to leave the Midwest and to return to California. Even though I had a good position with the railroad as a private secretary in their general offices in Cleveland, there was too much about my experiences which were depressing me. While I was on the West Coast during my brief naval experience, I became aware that life in the West was somewhat less oppressive for homosexuals than it had been in the Midwest. San Francisco, particularly, was more tolerant than any other place I had been, even though it was not the mecca for gay and lesbian people that it has now become. I decided to move to San Francisco, where I immediately embarked on a thirty-year career as a seafarer aboard merchant ships.

At some point during my seafaring career, I crossed the fine line between recreational, social drinking and pathological, excessive drinking. I became a full-blown alcoholic. Even though it is over nineteen years since I have taken a drink, I have not forgotten the nightmarish horror of alcohol addiction. My initial association with the only gay group of Alcoholics Anonymous in San Francisco, if not in the entire country, was the beginning of my open association with the gay community, in 1969, at the age of forty-nine. In addition to helping me with my drinking problem, they also taught me about something that I had forgotten even existed: real love and caring. This association with the gay community conferred on me a sense of belonging that I had never before experienced.

For the first time I felt the freedom to be who I was, and I was no longer willing to try to be someone I was not.

In much the same way that I was accepted by Gay AA, I was also welcomed into Dignity. They taught me to be who I am, and that I cannot be what some other person or institution thinks I should be. The gay or lesbian Catholic is involved in a two-front battle: with the Church because we are gay, and with the gay community because we are Catholic and fight tenaciously to remain so, in spite of the Church's continuing oppression. For my own part, this institution stripped me of my integrity once — it will never do so again.

Because of the support I have received from Gay AA and Dignity, I have regained my own sense of integrity and am proud to be a gay senior, slowing down perhaps, but not yet ready to withdraw from the fight for our rights. It is a real joy to know that my retirement years do not have to be spent in hiding as my formative years were.

Ready for new challenges, I applied for admission as an undergraduate and pursued a program in philosophy. I continued on a graduate level and received a master of arts degree from San Francisco State University at the age of sixty-two. I am starting on my second master's program now.

◆

The few noisy queers at Stonewall have multiplied beyond anyone's most optimistic expectations, and we proclaim to the world that we are here to stay. The AIDS epidemic and its predictable homophobic backlashes have bonded us ever more closely, as we support and care for those in our community who are suffering. We have been hurt before, and will be again, but we will never return to the subterranean caves of yesteryear.

I do not regret my past, for I believe I have done the best I could with the tools I had. But as someone who has spent much of his life in a tributary to the mainstream, knowing that I now belong to a community for which I care deeply — and which cares for me in return — has made the long wait worth it. Whenever the Supreme Navigator orders this old sailor to weigh anchor and cast off for the final voyage, it will be with the feeling that it has all been worthwhile.

Wilton Beggs

Revelation

Even now I remember my awakening as if it were yesterday, each detail precise, undiminished by the passage of time. How could I forget the most important day of my youth?

It was late August, 1950. I was sixteen that summer, and in those days Pine Mill was a sluggish East Texas town, smaller, more insular than now, almost forty years later. Human activity that hot afternoon was minimal. Only a few people moved about the square.

The courthouse in the center of the square dominated our town. It was an architectural nightmare of Gothic arches, corner towers, and false battlements. Ancient trees shaded its lawns. Beneath the trees were slatted benches, empty that afternoon except for three old men. A statue of a Confederate veteran stood behind the bench where the old men sat.

I was looking out a window of Moore's Drugstore when I saw Martin Deaver come out of a courthouse door with his usual long-legged swagger. I was instantly alert: Martin's angry scowl could mean trouble. Pine Mill's tall, good-looking football hero, Martin had been my neighbor since I was born. The Deavers were respectable. Martin's father was a successful merchant and a deacon in the Southern Baptist Church.

The son, however, was no saint. Eleven months older than I and more muscular, a natural foe of anyone who read books, Martin had evidenced a brash, almost cheerful contempt toward me for as long as I could remember. My first black eye at the age of seven came from his fist. Over the years other bruises were tokens of his displeasure. I had never won a fight with him, and I considered him a mental throwback to the Neanderthals. Yet our proximity in a small town made us inevitable associates. My father, a carpenter, had built the Deaver family home, and I shared a number of friends with Martin. We were in no way chums, but neither were we absolute enemies.

He's mad and hunting for someone, I thought as I watched Martin stride across the lawn in my direction. His handsome head was cocked angrily; I could see his chest rise and fall. I breathed a quick prayer that he would stay out of the drugstore. I had no doubt Martin — if his mood were foul enough — could create a pointless scene just for the drama.

"All I need is that bum getting me fired," I muttered.

I had good reason to be apprehensive. There were seldom enough dollars in my family, and to earn spending money I was working in the store that summer for Mr. Shale Moore. An acrimonious widower who knew I needed the job very much, Mr. Moore would take pleasure in blaming me for any disturbance Martin might cause.

I grunted with loathing as I watched Martin spit amber juice on the lawn. Forbidden cigarettes by the school football coach, Martin and some of his teammates had recently begun chewing tobacco. I thought it a disgusting vice, though several of the boys involved were among the more desirable young men in town.

My perception of my schoolmates' attractiveness I kept strictly private. Although at sixteen I knew where my sexual preference lay, I had found no way to act upon it. In my mind I was a pariah already, a latter-day brother of the biblical degenerates who had caused the destruction of Sodom.

Like most of my generation, I was unaware that there were, somewhere, people of my kind about whom I could feel pride. My horizon had never encompassed a gay writer, actor, or artist. I could not have imagined a gay lifestyle of any type. For me the millenniums of gay history, our enviable contribution to Western culture, our very *being,* was nonexistent. I had never heard of a homosexual publication, nor seen a motion picture that touched in any recognizable manner on the subject. No one had hinted to me that there might actually be organizations of gay people in my world. In truth, I did not know the word *gay* meant anything other than "merry." And that summer I was not merry.

At sixteen, though the son of loving and well-intentioned parents, I felt increasingly alone, racked by emotions I was sure no one of any worth had ever experienced. I thought myself unique in the worst sense of the word, and lived in real fear that Martin or someone of his caliber would discover my shameful secret. Should that happen, I could not fathom how I would continue my life.

As Martin was gathering the saliva in his mouth for another amber stream, I saw a girl walk past the bench where the three elderly men were sitting. Martin showed immediate interest in her. Glaring, his frown more pronounced than before, he stepped forward into a pool of sunlight. The newcomer did not notice him. Martin was almost hidden from her by the statue. She hurried on unheedingly, heels clicking on sun-dappled pavement.

Martin wore a look of incredulous outrage as his eyes followed the girl. A moment passed, then I watched him turn and head toward a telephone booth beside a courthouse door. The girl hurried on, and did not glance around until she reached the corner of the square. By this time Martin was inside the booth, his back to her.

On the shaded bench the three old men mumbled together and punched one another with sharp elbows. In a town where everyone knew his neighbor, and many were kin, such a flamboyant stranger was bound to cause comment.

The girl — for Pine Mill — was spectacular. Her figure was slender but feminine, her face aristocratic with a classic Greek nose and great brown eyes. Her hair was a dark auburn that fell below her shoulders. Rather tall, she held herself well, and each movement flowed into the next. Her red dress was garish, with a plunging neckline and fringed hem. Oversized jewelry gave her a tawdry appearance belied by the patrician face. In one hand she clutched a cardboard suitcase. I guessed her to be about twenty.

She waited for an automobile to pass, then started across the brick street just as Martin left the phone booth and quickly followed her. The girl pulled the drugstore door open and almost ran inside. The swirling blades of the ceiling fans stirred her hair as she let the door swing to with a spanking noise. Seeing the store had no customers, she gave me a hesitant glance. I realized she was frightened. Up close I saw her makeup had been applied in the lustrous fashion an actress might use. This emphasized even more the odd impression of bluff and innocence.

"Can I help you?" I remember saying inanely.

As she approached me I sensed something exotically knowable about the girl, but my mind could not identify it. I stepped behind the counter of the soda fountain and waited. She regarded me with a wary half-smile.

"I don't know why I did this," she whispered. "I'm scared silly. You don't recognize me?"

The words were breathless. Nonplused, I shook my head. She gave a laugh. Nearly my height, she stared at me apprehensively for several seconds.

"Maybe you know my kinfolks," she said at last, her voice husky. "The Askews?"

"The Southern Baptist preacher?" I began to understand why she seemed familiar. "You do favor his daughter. Betty's the prettiest girl in Pine Mill."

She hesitated. "Well, Betty's my cousin."

She moved forward in a self-conscious manner that struck me as slightly incongruous, suddenly rather clumsy. She pointed to a time chart on the wall behind me.

"I need a bus ticket. I have to get out of here!"

Like many small East Texas towns even today, Pine Mill had no genuine bus station. Buses pulled off the highway and stopped on the square. Passengers arrived at and departed from the sidewalk in front of the drugstore.

I ran a finger down the list of cities. "Where to?"

"The first bus out," she said flatly. I must have shown my perplexity, for she bit her lip and forced an unconvincing smile. "The bus to Dallas," she said, flushing.

Her nervousness was contagious. I stared at her with wonder, realizing how close she was to panic.

"What's wrong?" Not knowing why, I felt somehow involved. "Is Martin Deaver bothering you?"

She glared at me, the color draining from her cheeks. Her rather large hands were clenched. There was no sound except the creaking of the ceiling fans.

"Have you seen Martin?" she asked hoarsely.

Before I could speak we heard the slap of the drugstore

door. The girl winced, but did not turn as the thump of Martin's boots filled the room. I drew back from the counter involuntarily, for his face was a mask of rage.

The girl stood motionless as the footsteps came closer. Much taller than she was, Martin halted directly behind her. The rasp of his breathing was ominous. No one spoke. She stared ahead, at me, blank-faced, as if blocking out his presence.

He hit her, hard. The blow knocked her upon the counter. Her suitcase slipped from her hand, the clasps breaking open, male shirts and trousers spilling out. I was paralyzed by shock. Again Martin struck her, and she fell to the floor. An earring skidded over the tiles until it hit a wall and shattered. The girl lay inert, facedown, unprotesting.

Coming to my senses, I jumped over the counter and grabbed Martin's arm. "You'll hurt her bad!" I said in horror.

Martin's blue eyes were points of flame. His handsome face was slackjawed, hideous with a passion I could not read. He jerked in frustration as I fought to keep him from the girl.

"Stay out of this, fool," he said roughly. I clung to him to keep from being hurled aside. "You're too stupid to understand!"

The door at the rear of the room sprang open. Shale Moore, my employer, came running across the long expanse. Shale, in those days, was a fat, graceless old person with frowzy white hair and the disposition of a shrew. Seeing his wide-eyed indignation, I was sure my employment would soon be terminated. He rushed up to us and made ineffectual shushing motions with knobby hands.

"Goddamn bastards!" he yelled, for Shale was profane as most people in that era were not, and excessively ill-tempered. "Take your fighting outside!"

Shale was about to make further demands when he became aware of the girl. His eyes were bulging wider as Shale advanced and nudged her with his foot. The girl groaned and sat up. She leaned back against the counter painfully. A trickle of blood ran down her cheek from a superficial cut on the temple. The girl glowered at Martin, her fear apparently under control.

"Who's that?" said Shale. His wrinkled countenance was swathed in resentment. "What y'all been doing in my store?"

Martin did not answer. His eyes were locked with the girl's in an unreadable duel. Guarding myself watchfully, I loosened my grip on his arms and stepped back. He paid me no attention.

"Who is this woman?" Shale said stridently. "What's wrong with the bitch?"

"Don't y'all know Cary Askew?" Martin said with a sneer. "Take a good look."

His shirt damp with perspiration, Martin walked over to the girl and pulled at her hair. I was dumbfounded when the hair gave way and I saw Martin clutching a long auburn wig in his hand. Beneath the wig was the close-cropped blond head of a boy. The boy had a painted face and wore a gaudy red dress — and was, beyond any doubt, Cary Askew, Betty Askew's sixteen-year-old brother.

"What the hell?" said Shale Moore. "She's a fellow!"

I was gaping, unable to move. If a meteor had crashed through the ceiling I could not have been more astonished. I knew Cary Askew to be a quiet, diffident boy who made excellent grades in school and was something of a star during baseball season. He was my friend. I had "run" with him most of my life. Nothing in our past had prepared me for this.

"A dress," said Shale disbelievingly. "And stuffed tits! One of Preacher Askew's kids!"

Although I did not speak, I could not help sharing Shale's dismay. The situation was too bizarre for my limited experience. True to my upbringing, I had not penetrated Cary's disguise — mainly because it had never occurred to me that a man of our town could dress as a woman.

"A goddamn painted boy!" said Shale, terribly offended. "In that wig he looked like a woman ten years older!"

Martin wiped his mouth grimly. "He's sick, Mr. Moore. His sister told me about him a year ago. That's Betty's stage outfit he's got on."

"He must be nuts," said Shale. "I never heard of such a thing!"

Looking at Cary I remembered Betty Askew's costume for the high school play that previous May. She had portrayed a dancehall wench reformed by a noble rustic. Though a "moral" comedy, the play had been thought too daring by some in the community, and the Reverend Askew — a man of stern beliefs — had apologized later to his congregation for allowing his daughter's participation. The dress Cary had on, complete with jewelry, was Pine Mill's version of what a wanton should wear.

"I've been going with Betty since the tenth grade," Martin told Shale confidentially. "Brother Askew knows his son's crazy. When I saw that dress out there on the square, I phoned Betty, and she said both Cary and it were missing."

"Get that scum out of here," Shale snapped. He darted a sharp glance at the front window. "What if somebody sees him? What would folks say? The Askews were my late wife's cousins. This is pure shit!"

Shale made an imperious gesture to me, and I began shoving clothes back into Cary's suitcase. I felt numb, dazed by conflicting emotions, as I snapped the clasps and handed the suitcase to him. Digging into a pocket, I gave Cary my handkerchief to wipe the blood from his cheek.

"They think I'm crazy, so why not be?" he said. His voice was shaking, but altogether masculine as he looked at me squarely. "Why not give them a show?"

I felt myself turn crimson. In his mien was an implication of intimacy that was chilling. I was as embarrassed as if he had stripped me naked. I realized he knew.

"I'm not the only one in this town who's crazy," he said.

I drew back, appalled. Against my will I recalled with shamed vividness the nights Cary and I had spent together as buddies during the past year. Had I been so obvious, stealing my guilt-ridden glances as we undressed for bed? Had he, as I, experienced the confused and desperate needs I had suppressed?

"Take him in back," Shale said with disgust. "Wash the paint off and get him in shirt and pants. I'll call his daddy to come fetch him." He snorted. "Askew will *kill* the little punk."

Cary's face went white beneath the makeup. He got to his feet unsteadily.

"Let me alone," he said to Martin. "Martin, don't make things any worse."

"I can make it any way I want it, sonny." Martin tossed the wig behind the counter, grabbed Cary's wrist, and pulled him away. "Your pop expects me to whip you into a regular person."

I heard this with skepticism. Although Martin had dated Betty Askew for a couple of years, and his father was a leader in their church, I was sure Brother Askew disapproved of Martin, anyway. Martin's reputation extended beyond Pine Mill. Several escapades with wilder girls of the county, plus a rumor that he had fathered a baby, had made Martin a dubious candidate for marriage to a strict minister's daughter. But Betty was smitten. Despite his blatant unfaithfulness I knew Betty dated no one but him, and I thought it possible *she* had asked Martin to ride herd on her brother.

"I'll cure you yet, sissy," Martin taunted as he towed Cary along. He shook his fist in the smaller boy's face. "Here's the medicine for queers."

At this threat Cary gave such a hooting, cynical laugh that I jumped. "Hypocrite!" he said.

Cary's hysterical laughter was cut off as Martin slapped him. Martin shoved him through the door. It closed, and Shale and I were left with the silence of the room broken only by a murmur of ceiling fans.

"Holy Brother Askew thought my wife lowered herself marrying me," Shale chuckled. He hitched up his baggy trousers and walked to the telephone behind the counter. "I'll make that pious son of a bitch squirm."

I glanced about me in a daze. Mere minutes had passed since I had noticed Martin across the street. The afternoon sun had not moved perceptibly. Through the window I could still see the three old men sitting on their bench.

"Martin was mad before he spotted Cary," I said. "It was like he was already looking for him, Mr. Moore."

Taking the telephone receiver from its cradle, Shale fixed me with his gimlet stare. "Worry about *me* being mad, boy. If you want to keep working here, forget this. It's bad for business. The damn Askews are my meat."

I regarded the old man with open dislike. "Cary's my friend," I said shortly. "I wouldn't rat on a friend."

Shale's thin cackle was laden with innuendo. "I'll bet you wouldn't, sweetums." His face crinkled in scorn. "Anybody into that sort of shit is better off dead."

I don't think I have ever hated anyone so much as I did Shale Moore at that moment. It is the earliest encounters with heterosexual arrogance that hurt you the most.

"Quit gawking," Shale said gruffly. "I'll tell his pa to drive down the alley. I don't want my customers exposed to this crap. You help Martin get that queer into some decent clothes." His large-knuckled fingers began dialing the telephone. "Y'all have your *friend* ready when the preacher gets here."

Seething with resentment at his mocking tone, I went to the rear of the store. My hand was on the doorknob before the realization struck me that I was no longer alone in Pine Mill. The force of the notion was numbing.

Cary is too, I remember thinking to myself with awe. *A freak like me!* I had been floundering for so long with my forbidden desires, convinced no one else in the universe had my affliction – and now, without warning, I had discovered Cary Askew was a monster, also. The initial glimmering that someone in Pine Mill shared my secret was the closest I think I ever came to heaven.

I was shaking as I went into the darkened hallway and shut the door behind me. Water splashed in the restroom to my right. I moved forward quietly, then stopped for a while, gathering my confused thoughts. Minutes passed before voices became audible. Neither Martin nor Cary had yet detected my presence.

"Keep away from me, Martin," I heard Cary say, low. "I hate you."

I leaned against the wall, hardly breathing. I was so weak my knees threatened to buckle. Abruptly I guessed why Martin had been so upset even before he spied Cary on the courthouse lawn.

"You were with Andy Newcomb last night," Martin was saying furiously. "You were in Andy's car!"

The rank, sexual jealousy was unmistakable. In the dimness of the hall I shook my head like a prizefighter who has sustained a violent blow. Andy Newcomb was a married man in his midtwenties, the son of Pine Mill's mayor. At that moment I began to suspect dimensions to my restricted world I had never dreamed.

"If you don't leave me alone I'll tell them everything," Cary said hoarsely. "Daddy will beat me to a pulp, anyway." He paused, while the noise of running water diminished. "How'd you like Betty to know?"

There was a quick, keen report, and I knew Martin had hit Cary again. I clenched my fists, longing to harm Martin in any way I could.

"You filthy pansy," Martin spat. "I'm trying to help you!"

"Sure," said Cary bitterly. "That's why you can't stand me to even talk to another guy."

Before Martin could strike Cary again I slammed the wall with my elbow. The water shut off, and I could sense them listening.

"You're a coward, Martin," Cary said softly into the silence. "At least I'm honest with myself."

The door banged open, and Martin was scowling at me, the light of the restroom flooding around him. I thought for a moment he would attack me, for his manner was that of a cornered animal. With a baleful curse he swung and went out into the alley. I heard his footsteps hurrying away.

It was some time before I could summon enough courage to walk to the restroom door. When I moved into the light Cary was standing beside the washbasin, his wounded eyes level with mine. He had removed the makeup and jewelry, and was clothed in jeans and a plaid shirt. While I watched he pushed his feet into a pair of scuffed loafers. The red dress and padded bra lay crumpled beside the open suitcase. He looked very vulnerable but not at all feminine.

"I figured it was you," he said. "I've sure made a mess, haven't I? Damn, I don't even *want* to be a girl."

His face was pale and scared. I put out my hand. He gripped it tightly.

"I don't understand," I remember saying, trying to puzzle it out. "Why'd you dress up like that?"

"Honest, I don't really know." He managed a self-deprecating smile, and I recall thinking him the bravest, most beautiful boy I had ever seen. "Maybe to show them I'm as bad as they think because it's the stuff they accuse me of." He shrugged. "Maybe just to show Daddy I'm not afraid of his rotten Hell."

I caught my breath, and the dam burst: "Well, I don't care if go there, either!"

With a grateful sigh I will never forget, Cary put his arm around me. "I've tried to tell you a dozen times this year," he said. I remember his kissing me then, and the frantic way my heart pounded against my chest as if it would burst. "I *knew* you were like me."

"At least your dad won't be with us in Hell," I said.

He chuckled and held me tighter. "A place like that can't be all bad, can it?"

I think those minutes with Cary Askew, in Pine Mill the summer I was sixteen, must have been the happiest of my life.

Guy-Oreido Weston

Crossing Bridges

 One Sunday afternoon in the spring of '83, a friend and I arrived in Philadelphia from our insulated suburban communities in search of some sort of gay social activity. As we drove through Center City, we noticed dark lavender newspaper boxes on several corners with *Gay News* written on them. "Maybe we can find something in the *Gay News,*" I told my friend. But both of us were afraid to be seen buying a gay newspaper in broad daylight. We argued and eventually flipped a coin. I lost. As inconspicuously as possible, I approached the box, dropped in my three quarters, took the paper, and walked back to my car, hoping that I had not been noticed.

That was three years ago...

This past summer I befriended a visitor from Latin America who was so excited by the freedom of expression that he witnessed among gay men in Greenwich Village that he could not wait to try it himself. One evening as we walked down a residential street in downtown Philadelphia, he took my hand and held it. I did not know whether to hold his hand or not. As we walked down the street I thought: *Four months ago, I moved from suburbia to "gay" downtown Philly. I have a "gay" job, working for the city's AIDS Control Program. I write for the gay press and spend very little time projecting conventional heterosexual masculinity for the sake of peers, co-workers, or family who are too narrow-minded to accept who I really am. I am not going to get fired from my job if I am "discovered." Is there any reason to be afraid to be myself?* NO! I put my thoughts aside, braced myself, and continued to walk along talking to my friend – with one eye scanning in front of us waiting for a homophobe to hurl a brick or yell, "Faggot." The first few blocks were pretty empty, but we eventually reached South Street, an avant-garde social gathering place full of restaurants, shops, and people who stay around until well after midnight.

Although South Street is the one place in Philly where anything goes, I was slightly apprehensive, because there were so many people around. Surprisingly, nobody seemed to notice us. A couple of people snickered or said things under their breath, but no one gave us any reason to feel the least bit intimidated. The most noticeable reaction came from a gay friend of mine who did a double take and looked after us in disbelief as we walked by the restaurant where he worked.

The next day, out of sheer curiosity, I decided that we would walk down Chestnut Street, a main thoroughfare in the business district of the city. It was about noon and the sidewalks were full of people from the surrounding stores and offices on their lunch breaks. Again, we failed to elicit any overt expressions of disgust, and the majority of people seemed not to notice us, although we did get a few more stares and one or two verbal insults that were not loud enough to warrant any concern.

This experience caused me to re-examine my values, but not to the extent that I considered constantly flaunting my sexual orientation to see how much I could get away with. If I continued to parade proudly down Chestnut Street, eventually some belligerent anti-gay behavior would cross my path, and I do not want to walk around wondering when it's going to occur.

On the other hand, I no longer consider it necessary to keep the real me a prisoner inside myself. I don't have to be selectively invisible or take great pains to conceal my identity for fear that the wrong person might find out. I can just be myself. If someone asks, I'll tell them. But I don't have to announce it to everyone that comes by, any more than I announce anything else about myself. My attraction for men goes back almost as far as I can remember. When I was four years old, an older boy threatened to take me and four of my playmates into his bathroom individually to search our pants to see if we had stolen a lost toy. I was disappointed, because my turn never came. There was something exciting about the prospect of that older boy going into my pants. By the time I was seven, I was going into a neighbor's garage for he and I to compare penises and poke them against each other. When I was ten, I attempted anal sex with another boy for the first time. At thirteen, I had my first ejaculation and realized soon thereafter that this same-sex attraction was not just a passing thing. I would have to work hard to become "normal." I had five sex partners throughout childhood and early adolescence. Although these sexual experiences had been infrequent, I knew what I wanted and thought it was wrong. Since my father was in the air force, I was spending most of my free time in children's activities at the local Protestant chapel set up for military personnel and their families. It was very clear to me that God wanted me to be an all-American, patriotic, macho, sexist, Christian little boy. And I knew that he would make me just that, if I would deny myself and follow him.

My father's career took me away from my last sex partner and friend. For the rest of my adolescence, I remained celibate while I attempted to rid myself of this "deviant sexual orientation."

Following the faith of my upbringing, I chose to attend a middle-of-the-road Christian liberal arts college after high school. Even though no one at the college knew my secret, I was encouraged to feel guilty and seek change, because of the negative depictions of homosexuality in Bible study and in adolescent psychology class.

During this time a movement that called itself Radical Evangelical was getting a lot of publicity in Christian magazines. This school of thought was known for an unusual preoccupation with social issues.

One of the issues that they were "radical" about was a "new" look at homosexuality and the scriptures. Frequently, they were less judgmental and some were even supportive and offered resources such as psychological support to persons such as myself. Initially, I was slightly suspicious of this movement's outlook on homosexuality, because it contradicted my literalist interpretation of the Bible. Eventually I became excited by this new perspective and involved myself in other "unpopular" causes they advocated. With a similar concern about issues such as U.S. involvement in Central America, I decided to finish my undergraduate work at a theological seminary in Costa Rica.

While Costa Rica is accurately reputed to be the most peaceful democratic nation in Latin America, it is surrounded by political turmoil resulting primarily from its northern border with Nicaragua. It was rewarding to be involved in a Christian movement that saw its mission as helping to put an end to the blatant exploitation of a people by Nicaragua's

Anastasio Somoza Debayle — the ruthless dictator who looted his country before being overthrown by the Sandinistas. It was evident, though, that people fighting to achieve the most basic tenets of "life, liberty, and the pursuit of happiness" would not get around to dealing with an issue such as homosexuality. As a gay friend of mine from Nicaragua once put it: "There will never be a gay liberation movement here as long as people are fighting for their lives."

Of course, the absence of a visible gay movement did not mean that there were any fewer gay people around. By a stroke of luck, my roommate at the seminary was gay. Unfortunately, our fun did not last for long, and eventually we stopped being friends. "God would get us if we didn't quit it," as far as he was concerned.

I knew better. After having tried to fight off my passions for several years and having learned to read the Bible in a different light, I had concluded that God created me as I am; that my sexual orientation was normal and that I could love a man without feeling guilty. Since my roommate thought such words were blasphemous, I decided to leave him alone.

Frustrated and lonely, I decided to resort to the popular cruising area in the central park. The equivalent of less than five dollars bought me a friendly hustler and another two dollars and thirty-five cents paid for a hotel room in the Zona Roja, the Red Zone, for a few hours. Eventually, I made two regular "friends," who despised each other, because I paid such good money and I would only see one of them per day. If I'd had any sense I would have "passed," allowing my friends to think that I was a black Latin American, instead of telling them that I was North American. Then I would have only had to pay about two dollars and fifty cents for tricks, instead of the "expensive" five-dollar rate for American visitors.

This was fun for about two months. Eventually, I could not stand it anymore. I had always wanted to live out my sexual life the same way "conventional" couples do — in a covenant relationship, according to my religious convictions. My hustler friends and I had actually become great buddies, but they were still seventy-five percent money motivated.

Feeling distracted from school, I returned to the United States to work out the struggles of my sexual orientation with the intention of returning to Latin America as soon as I got myself together.

Soon after returning to this country, I began to seek out some of the gay religious groups I had heard about previously. After my first meeting, I followed most of the members into the gay bar next door. I was appalled. I could not shift gears so quickly. The brand of Christianity that I had come to know as a child would never permit that the after-church social would be held in a bar. But I was glad I went. I ran into a very popular student from the Christian college that I had attended. His lover was a prominent ex–staff member. That evening I found out that several members of our fraternity were gay, as well as other friends, but we were all afraid to admit it at the time, because we thought we were sinful. We could have eliminated so much of our struggle and loneliness if we had only been honest, but our religious tradition would not allow it. Unknown to all of us, we had the makings of an underground gay student organization — with a faculty advisor, too. This drove home the fact that I was not the only gay Christian in the world. At that same bar I met ministers, a popular local gospel disc jockey, and even a Grammy award–winning gospel music star.

"There is something to be said for these gospel queens," a friend of mine once said sarcastically. "How many choirloft spaces, organ benches, and pulpits would be empty if they all stayed home?"

◆

It was a few months after this experience that I arrived in Philadelphia on a Sunday afternoon and was afraid to be seen buying a *Gay News*. I had fully accepted who I was and decided to work on being as happy as I possibly could, but there was still a lot to lose by becoming openly gay. I would surely jeopardize my job. At the age of twenty-four, I was still living with my parents. They would probably become rude to my friends and begin to censor my telephone calls. My conservative friends would disown me. I had become a linguist and aspired to pursue my Latin American interests through an international organization such as the United Nations or the Organization of American States. Would I risk such an opportunity for the sake of becoming an openly gay man?

For three years I lived as a selectively invisible gay man leading a double life, but eventually I moved out of my parents' house. Then I reserved my invisibility only for family and work. Even after I told my mother, I was forced to remain closeted in the presence of family to avoid friction.

When I began to write for the gay press and subsequently went to work for the city's AIDS Control Program, it suddenly occurred to me that my motives for being an invisible gay man had ceased to exist. Having moved into Center City to be close to work, I was living in a gay neighborhood, working in a situation where my sexual orientation was often an asset and a known fact to my employers. Seeing my name in print for the first time in a gay publication felt very good. But sometimes I forgot that the rest of the world was not like this gay ghetto that I lived and worked in. Everyone was not free to be as visible as I was.

That message was driven home when I decided to stop working for the AIDS program and go to graduate school. Would I be a different person when I was uptown at school than when I was downtown at home? What if I became active in the gay student organization and the chairperson of my academic department found out? Would that motivate her to choose one of the other three equally qualified students for that one available graduate assistantship? Suppose I want to apply for a job there when I graduate?

Some individuals may choose to forego open acknowledgment of their sexual orientation in order to fight another unpopular cause, such as my friend in Nicaragua. I know someone else who feels he must remain closeted because he is an elementary school teacher without tenure.

That might work well for them. They would probably argue that it is a matter of dire necessity and that it is well worth the sacrifice. Be that as it may, I can no longer deny who I am. I have no specific strategy for my future – I will cross each bridge when I come to it.

Scot Roskelley

Coming Out to My Wife

It was one of those sultry summer evenings — the kind you long for in the middle of a January ice storm — the kind Portland is so famous for. After finishing dinner, our five-year-old son scurried outside to join the neighbors' kids, leaving his mother and me at the dinner table.

My wife Julie had begun seeing a counselor five months earlier and was dealing with a bad case of "identity crisis." She was changing dramatically — turning into a person of her own making rather than a mirror image of her parents or husband. And as she changed, so did our relationship. I was at a loss as to how to relate to this new person, this person who for all her change seemed to still be suffering emotional agony.

Observing all of this caused my own introspection. Who was I? What did I really want out of a relationship? And was I getting it, or would I ever get it?

Over the months while Julie searched for her new identity, I built a protective wall around myself. As she tried to penetrate my secure fortress, she became even more frustrated. Communication had reached a standstill over the weeks, and here we were at the dinner table.

"What is going to become of us?" I asked, fearful of the consequences of this conversation. This was the first time I had ever cast doubt on our future together.

Julie proceeded to describe the defenses she perceived I was building, concluding with the recommendation that I, too, seek counseling. Having watched what Julie had gone through, I was well aware that psychologists probe into every recess of your inner being. If I were to deal with my tangled emotions, it would mean bringing everything out in the open.

"Julie," I said, "the things I might have to deal with as a result of counseling will no doubt involve you and are things you shouldn't have to deal with until you've finished counseling and are in a better emotional state."

Worried that the proverbial cat was on its way out of the bag, I began clearing dishes from the table as a diversion.

It didn't work.

All the while, Julie pursued this same vein. "If there are things you're going to bring out, I don't see why we can't work on them now. What could they be? What are you talking about?" she asked.

Five minutes of a cat-and-mouse game ensued. I was washing the dishes, and Julie was drying.

"Scot," she asked while drying a drinking glass, "are you gay?

The question brought on a sudden wave of nausea. And I immediately realized that my response could dramatically change the course of my life in the next hour, the next month, and even the next year. The effects would be long-standing. And they meant change.

I was tired of change. I had been riding an emotional roller coaster for four months now watching her change. I was looking for an end to change, not a beginning.

Yet, years before, I had resolved that if she were to ask, I must give the honest answer.

Panic squeezed every muscle. The few seconds spent rationalizing my decision seemed like hours. And I became acutely aware that to hesitate much longer was to confirm her suspicion.

"Let's finish the dishes first and then sit down and talk," I answered. The following ten minutes in the kitchen were, and no doubt will always be, the longest ten minutes of my life.

With the kitchen clean, we sat on the couch and I poured out my story. I had felt attracted to men as long as I could remember, but to act on that feeling was impossible in my mind. My religious upbringing had taught me that God frowned on homosexual activity. And besides, as a youth, I lived in a rednecked town tucked away in the California Sierras. Homosexuality was akin to things like murder and incest in the eyes of the community. I was quite certain I was the only one in the entire county of 22,000 people to feel the way I felt.

I attended a church-operated liberal arts college in the midseventies, which helped reinforce the "sin concept" of homosexuality. Fulfilling the expectations of society, I dated women throughout my college years, assuming that my desire for men would subside.

One day, I met a woman who lit "something" within me. It was instant enchantment. Julie had the same zest for life that I had. And we enjoyed so many of the same things. As time rolled by, I came to the conclusion that there would never be anyone whose company I could enjoy more than hers.

And, miracle of miracles, she even awakened a spark of sexual desire in me. At last, these homosexual feelings would be put to rest.

In 1977 we were married and moved to Los Angeles.

Time passed, and those feelings didn't disappear. Instead, they grew stronger. In October of 1979, while my wife was six months pregnant with our son, I realized these feelings were here to stay. I knew I had control over how I responded, but I had no control over the feelings themselves. It was then that I finally accepted that I was gay.

On the heels of this realization, I had my first gay sexual experience. Afterward, I never again doubted my true sexual orientation.

I became active in a local organization of professional gay men. For the first time, I saw gay men who were just like me. They were teachers, doctors, priests, and architects. Where were the sex-crazed perverts society had warned me about? These were decent, respectable, hard-working people. Seeing them helped me accept myself in a way nothing else could.

What was most difficult to accept was how I could reconcile my homosexuality with my marriage. I loved my wife. I thought she was a great person and couldn't ever conceive of finding anyone, male or female, that I could be more compatible with. The only problem with her was the packaging. And that was a significant problem.

Months wore on. There were more sexual encounters. And then, I was transferred to the Pacific Northwest. Absorbed in the tedium of a new job, acquiring new friends, and raising a son, the sexual encounters came to a halt. But the acceptance of my sexuality remained the same. So did the attraction to men.

Several years later, Julie and I became acquainted with a man named David. I'd met him through my business contacts as a public relations director. I had strong suspicions that he was gay, and after several months and a visit to his apartment, I was certain of it. A quote on his refrigerator, "They condemn that which they do not understand," was all I needed to see.

Weeks later, I confessed my own homosexuality to him and my hunch about David was confirmed. Over time, we became close friends, strictly platonic, and drew Julie into our friendship. It was like one of those tight threesomes you see in the movies. We did everything together, went everywhere together ... to the point that it might have appeared odd to outsiders.

We shared so much.

But there was one secret we both kept camouflaged from Julie – our sexuality. And while she couldn't put her finger on it, she knew there was something about this relationship she wasn't sharing equally. There were times when she felt like an outsider among us – like when we were served by a good-looking waiter or every time Mark Harmon appeared in a beer commercial.

Eventually, we felt it was necessary for David to divulge his sexuality. And Julie, who had never before had any close association with a gay person, went through the typical processing of this revelation. First came the questions: "How long have you felt this way?" "Did you choose to be this way?" "Are you sure about this?"

Then came the uneasiness. David was a person she liked a lot ... even loved. Yet, he was something she had always decided she didn't approve of. Either her opinion of David had to change, or her opinion of homosexuality had to change.

David and I watched her assimilate the messages. We studied her reactions over the next few days and weeks. We knew this might be a precursor to my eventual coming out to Julie.

In time, she became comfortable with David's homosexuality. She read more on the subject. She watched talk shows on TV. And she became an ardent defender of the gay cause.

This change in her views on homosexuality triggered rethinking of many of her long-standing values and was the catalyst for her beginning counseling. Over a period of six months, she changed considerably. The person I once knew no longer existed. Yet, the new person was still not fully developed. The "old Julie" and the "new Julie" were at war with each other. The transition period was long, and the effect on our relationship was immense.

To say that she took the news that I was gay with "the bat of an eye" would be a lie. However, the road had been paved with David. She knew that she could love a significant other who was gay. She knew she wasn't "less of a woman" because I was gay. Now, she was faced with whether she could love a husband, a sexual partner, who was gay, and continue a contractual relationship with that person.

Interestingly, my coming out to Julie improved our communication and served as a vehicle to tear down barriers we had built over the preceding months.

This was a crucial turning point in my life. I was at a fork in the road where I could say, "I love you, but I want out of the marriage so I can pursue a more ideal relationship with someone of my own sex."

Or I could say, "I love you and will repress sexual feelings, remaining faithful to you forever."

Or I could say, "I love you and want to make the marriage work, but I also want my sexual freedom."

I loved Julie. About that, there was no doubt. We had made it through bad times and good times. We shared many similar interests. And until recently, we had always communicated openly and resolved conflict well. I couldn't conceive of finding anyone I could be more compatible with. Thoughts ran through my mind of searching for the perfect man the rest of my life and ending up lonely because I never found him.

We discussed the future over and over again. The outcome was that we both loved each other. Julie felt she couldn't compel me to cloister my sexuality, and I didn't want to. We decided to pursue our relationship, taking it one day at a time. Neither of us knew of any other married couples that had remained together once one of them had announced his or her homosexuality. Yet, we were willing to forge what to us appeared to be a new trail.

We sought as much information and input as possible, talking with a gay priest, a gay counselor, and members of the local chapter of Parents and Friends of Lesbians and Gays. We discovered a professional couple with children, where the man is gay, that has remained happily married for over twenty years. We also discovered a family with a husband, a wife, and the wife's lesbian lover and her three children. While many in the gay community are skeptical about the success of a relationship such as Julie's and mine, they have been extremely supportive of our giving it a try. The love and concern shown for us has been overwhelming.

I am currently involved with another married man who has two children. Ours is a fairly new relationship. My wife is aware of this man's presence in my life, but does not want details. His wife is aware of his sexual orientation, but not of his current involvement with another man. Juggling two relationships is not easy, and it may not work forever. I could fall deeply in love with this man and feel the need to leave. She could decide she has compromised herself by remaining with a gay husband and leave.

Neither Julie nor I know what the future holds. Nonetheless, we are committed to our love for each other. Life is a process, and whether or not a marriage contract binds us together in the coming years, that love and concern for each other will always remain.

Robert Boucheron

Smitty

From public high school in Schenectady, New York, I went to Harvard College, with a vague idea of going on to medical school. My roommate for three years was Leigh, from Philadelphia – premed, a biochemistry "concentrator," in the jargon of Harvard, and, like me, a musician. At the start of the fall semester of our junior year, we were informed that because of overcrowding, a third man would be joining us. Philippe was originally from Haiti, by way of New York. The accident of interracial living made us all look progressive in 1972.

As upperclassmen, we had advanced to the luxury of a two-bedroom suite, with a private bath, and a working fireplace in the living room, all overlooking the street approach to Eliot House, with its tiny circular drive. Now the living room became Philippe's room. Actually, we offered to flip for it, but he insisted. He was as quiet and suburban as we were.

In the course of getting acquainted, I discovered that Philippe and I both played clarinet. He was out of practice, though. In fact, he wanted to sell his instrument. A notice in the vaulted entrance of Eliot House, called "the archway," produced a buyer, a sophomore who thought that taking up a wind instrument might be just the thing. I demonstrated it for him. Lessons? Yes, I could teach him once a week, for a nominal fee. We agreed to meet the next Tuesday night.

James Smith possessed a name so generic that there was a national Jim Smith Club, with reunions and a newsletter. He preferred the nickname Smitty. Our first lesson, in a chilly basement practice room, revealed that he could not read music, could not keep a steady beat, and was short of breath. He smoked cigarettes, which was part of the problem. We started with the basics: do re mi, tapping with a foot, and breathing with the diaphragm. I placed my hand on his abdomen and squeezed. He giggled. Who could have foreseen the result?

Given Smitty's lack of musical aptitude, and my headlong fascination with him, lessons degenerated into giddy talk. An English concentrator like me, he likewise attended the public schools. Unlike me, he hailed from a working-class area of Los Angeles. Brains and a considerable degree of charm earned him a scholarship. Naive enthusiasm carried him along. One year ahead, I gave him my opinion on introductory courses, and sold him the required books at half price. As classes got under way, Smitty skipped practicing, then abandoned the clarinet lessons.

By that time, I was a goner. I refused payment for the few lessons we had, and for the many we did not. We saw each other often in the dining hall, in the archway, and walking around Cambridge. I was conscious of the pleasure of his company, and of a desire to give. But why was the pleasure so keen, and what did I want to give? Smitten by Smitty, I was too dazed to know what had happened.

Soon it became painfully clear that he had many interests other than me, and joy gave way to despair. An "A" student during my sophomore year, I now struggled to keep up. Organic chemistry reduced me to tears, and not from the fumes in the laboratory. I nearly failed the course, instead receiving my first "D." I dropped out of the concert band, where I played first chair or solo. Weepy and miserable, I tried to slip into the dining hall early or late, so as to avoid Smitty. Catching up with me once, he asked why I was behaving oddly. What could I say — that I had fallen in love with him?

Experience is a great teacher. I learned, for example, that the romantic cliches repeated in movies and popular songs could be literally true. My bookish adolescence, untroubled by girls and rebellion, did not mean that I was a cold, heartless person. Here I was, suffering along with the best of them. I learned that love is blind — that the beloved may be unremarkable, even unsuitable, and yet magically attractive. And I reflected on the unfairness of the situation, that love may go unrequited.

Oddly enough, the fact that the object of my affection was male did not come as a surprise. Small for my age, and no good at sports, I had loathed and feared gym class. Yet I was curious about grown men. The photographs of men's clothing in the Sears Roebuck catalogue had called for repeated bouts of careful study. On the street or on the silver screen, men got closer attention than ostensibly sexy women. And surreptitiously, I had read a *Reader's Digest* article on "homosexuals," as though they were an obscure tribe in the Amazon jungle. But I had no sex life, no deep yearning, no fantasy scene to play out.

Once on a plane trip — back from Boston after my Harvard admission interview, in fact — I sat next to a hairdresser. He was a bit peculiar, but friendly. He said that his lady customers told him their most intimate secrets as he shampooed and curled. Their husbands, getting wind of this, somehow leaped to the conclusion that the hairdresser was having affairs with their wives. But if they only knew! There was absolutely no reason to be jealous, none! Somehow, without asking, I knew why.

The word *gay* was coming into use, but as yet I had no inkling of its political significance. I did not know any homosexual men, had never seen or heard of a gay bar, and did not even know the range of sexual acts available to consenting adults. Harvard had a gay student group, but it led a shadowy existence, and I did not think of myself that way. True, the Harvard's Hasty Pudding Theatricals were perhaps the longest-running drag show in the United States. But that fell more in the realm of clubs, high jinks, and student pranks.

So, in the face of an unpleasant reality — my attachment to Smitty — I retreated to books. In the dim recesses of Lamont Library, I discovered E.M. Forster and Christopher Isherwood. These two authors became my idols, and I read with fervor. They did not, of course, contribute any hard information as to sex. But their picture of intense male friendships, especially in a university setting, held vast appeal. Fiction, of course, but it was something to cling to. I cast myself in the role of a brilliant, sensitive undergraduate, with an unspeakable problem, and I suffered on.

In all, the affair was to last for five years. I did not remain uniformly depressed during that entire span of time. My grades improved somewhat, and I graduated on schedule. But I took as light a course load as I could, and devoted the remaining time to reading a wide range of world literature. Known for playing in the concert band, I was asked to play in pit orchestras for musical shows, of which Harvard produced a great many. I won a prize established more than a century earlier, of which Harvard also had a great many, "for a verse translation of an ode of Horace." And I walked for miles along the Charles River and into Boston.

I had friends, most of whom lived in Eliot House, and Leigh, my roommate. But Leigh and I did not talk much. In truth, we had little in common. I did not confide in him, and when he started dating girls, I saw even less of him. Philippe left after one semester. The overcrowding had eased, and he found better quarters.

A friend who lived in Lowell House, Ralph, not only shared many of my courses, but was clever, and interesting in a way I could not define. I sought him out, and tried to draw closer, but Ralph did not know what to make of me. Or he did know, and preferred to keep his distance. In any case, he was one of the brightest students in our class, a hard worker, headed for graduate school and a university career.

About this time, the movie version of *Cabaret* appeared, with Liza Minelli, Michael York, and Joel Grey. Not only was it based on stories by Isherwood, my hero, but the sexual ambiguities were fascinating. Uncharacteristically, I returned to see the movie again and again. Ralph saw both the Broadway show and the movie. He too was fascinated, but in talking about it, neither of us got personal. As I found out later, he was being coy. As for me, I failed to connect the images of decadent Berlin nightlife with my own life, or with Smitty.

Smitty, meanwhile, acquired a girlfriend. Coeducational living had started on a small scale during my sophomore year, as a few Radcliffe women moved into the Harvard dorms. The idea was that men and women would inhabit separate rooms. Maureen was one of these pioneers, and she moved into Eliot House. With no particular rules or enforcement, couples quietly formed, pushed twin beds together, moved clothing into the same closet, and books onto the same shelf. Smitty and Maureen became such a couple. She was pretty and athletic — she was on the intercollegiate water polo team — and she had a gentle, self-effacing manner. I had no feeling toward Maureen one way or the other. But when, from my window,

I saw them leave the dorm, their bodies so entwined that it must have been difficult to walk, I felt a pang.

Smitty remained the emotional focus of my life. While school was in session, we saw each other occasionally. During vacations, we wrote letters. He valued my friendship, and I tried not to pester him unduly with attention. But it was necessary at times for him to lie, to tell me for example that he had to write a paper, when in fact he was going to ride bicycles with Maureen. It was inevitable, at such times, for me to feel hurt.

Yet he once described how he was picked up on the bank of the Charles River, by a man who took him home, plied him with beer and a joint, and then tried to take advantage of him. He presented this story as a narrow escape. I wondered, though, what he thought the man had in mind, why Smitty had gone as far as he did, and what it was about Smitty that made the man try to seduce him. Did Smitty quite understand what he was about? Was he a cocktease?

What did Smitty owe me, if anything? Or, in platonic terms, what is the responsibility of the beloved to the lover? I thought about this question for years, and I still do. It seemed at the time that Smitty got off scot free, that the rules gave him a clear advantage, and me no leverage. My case was hopeless, and it would be better to forget about him. Indeed, I longed for the day when I would.

After the organic chemistry fiasco, I gave up the idea of medical school, but did not replace it with an alternate plan. Teaching English seemed like a possibility, if only by default. I had written some poetry, had one poem published in the Harvard literary magazine, and took a poetry writing seminar with Elizabeth Bishop. But I had no idea of becoming a writer. Law school looked utterly tedious. What other options were there? Almost until graduation in June, I was adrift.

At that point, I heard about a job opening in the university development office, to complete a set of reports on foundations and charitable trusts. I applied, interviewed, and was offered the job. It would start in July.

I found a place to live, a room in an apartment on Dana Street with some graduate students. The development office staff turned out to be eccentric, if not certifiable, but the job was not too demanding. I was still in Cambridge, and still playing in pit orchestras. I saw Smitty from time to time, with at least one long period of abstinence. He sometimes took the initiative in our getting together. On one occasion, as we sat at a sidewalk cafe, I raged about the characters at the office. Smitty brought me up short by saying that he did not need to listen to my problems.

This was also the time when Richard Nixon was forced out of office. At an "impeachment party" in the Eliot House laundry room, I watched him exit the White House on television, as Smitty joked that Nixon would now turn his attention to "penal reform." We had been lucky in the selective service lottery, and had been spared the nightmare of Vietnam. But we hated Republicans as an article of faith, and Nixon because he looked evil.

Some months into my writing job, I decided that I ought to pursue a favorite childhood activity, namely building. I would become an architect. This would mean going to graduate school, a prospect I did not relish. Nor was it a safe bet that I would get in, with a background in English. Never mind that I knew nothing about the practice of architecture. I filled out applications, solicited recommendations, and scratched together the required portfolio. I got into Yale.

Smitty took the news calmly. Maybe it was not such an achievement, maybe he was preoccupied. Soon after, he graduated, and won a traveling fellowship. For the moment, though, he returned to Los Angeles, where he taught adult education for a year. He had done this one or two summers, and derived great satisfaction from teaching. He had an apartment, and friends from high school. His letters tended to dwell on feelings, current reading, and poverty, with frequent announcements of reform. He would quit smoking, he would eat only rice and vegetables, he would keep a journal.

That summer, 1975, I stayed in the apartment on Dana Street. I quit my job prematurely, and had little to do, other than take a course in drawing that Yale demanded. In the fall, I found an apartment in New Haven — actually a room with a shared bath and kitchen — and started a three-year program for the degree of Master of Architecture. The first-year class was small, about thirty students, all together in a large studio. We all took the same courses, and we all socialized as a unit, despite the fact that several students were married. It was a unique experience in group behavior, but did not, of course, address all my needs.

The next fall, 1976, Smitty took his fellowship money to Cambridge, England, where he entered Jesus College. He changed flights in Boston, and I drove up to meet him for the weekend. Nervous, I got very drunk on vodka Saturday night. It was late, warm with a hint of the chill to come, and we stood on the flat roof of a house on Beacon Hill. In tears, I confessed, and received a big hug. He then slept with his girlfriend from Los Angeles, and I slept on her living room floor, where I could hear them humping. By Sunday morning, if anything had been stirred up or settled, Smitty did not let on. Sick, hysterical, I just wanted to leave.

Despite a disturbing dream I had of Smitty's death, he arrived safely in England. The climate and the tutorial system did not suit him, so he traveled after all, through Europe and to Israel, where he met an American woman named Jennifer. He followed her to Rome, where she was studying art. There they stayed till spring, 1977, when her year abroad was up, and Smitty's father died.

Meanwhile, I slowly got a grasp of architectural design. During the second year, a classmate told me that she had met a friend of mine at her church. A Harvard friend, in fact. Ralph? But he was Jewish. Not anymore. She obtained his phone number, I called, and we caught up.

Ralph had spent two years at Oxford, where he earned "their" undergraduate degree. While in England, he also came out – he and a few other gay students had "liberated" a college tea dance. He returned to America for a graduate program at Yale in comparative literature. There, under the influence of Yale historian and gay Catholic John Boswell, he converted to Christianity.

Naturally, I told Ralph about my long, unhappy passion for Smitty. Naturally, he told me to flush it. But Ralph was himself stuck in a hopeless affair. "Do as I say, not as I do," he ruefully advised.

Smitty flew to Los Angeles to settle his father's estate, which amounted to an old car, not pretty, but driveable. Jennifer joined him there, and they set off across America. Early on, they considered a swing up to New Haven. But after weeks on the road, they headed straight for Washington, D.C., where her family lived. Marriage was said to be imminent. Smitty still wanted to see me, though. He suggested that we meet approximately halfway, in New York.

It would have been easy enough for me to take the train, but I refused. "If you want to see me, you can come here," I wrote. I felt slighted, and in no mood to accommodate. Smitty telephoned on a Saturday morning, as I was spring cleaning.

We argued, but I used this trip as a test, and stood firm. We did not meet in New York, or anywhere else.

Smitty wrote a letter, rambling as usual through feelings and resolves for the future. I did not answer. He wrote once more, months later. The wedding fell through, he returned to England, but was no happier than before. How tiresome — Smitty was a bore!

The spell was lifted. The fall of 1977, in downtown New Haven, I walked around the block three times, and then into the door of a gay bar called Partners. Within minutes, a stranger bought me a beer, and an hour later took me home. It may not have been much fun, but he was a good sport.

New Haven had another gay nightspot called Les Oubliettes, also known as the Dungeon. Located underground, decorated with artificial stalactites, decorative shackles, and a large greenish aquarium, it boasted a disco dance floor and a back room, lit by a dim red bulb. I went to this bar too. One Saturday night in December, I met the man who would become my lover. He was slight, had fair pageboy hair, wore blue jeans and a plaid flannel shirt, and said little. A huge bunch of keys jangled from a belt loop.

"Are you a janitor?"

"No," he smiled.

Lights began to flash, as the next song started.

"Would you care to dance?"

"I don't, as a rule. But for you, I'll make an exception."

He did, for the first and last time. Never again would the disco beat entice him. He introduced me to magazines, leather, lubricants, opera, and a whole new cast of characters. We moved to New York, where we lived in a brick shoebox on West Twenty-first Street. We bought a subscription to the ballet.

But that is another story.

Jim Baxter

First-Class Mail

In the summer of 1974, as I looked forward to my twenty-first birthday, the idea of "coming of age" meant only one thing to me: "coming out." I wanted to be up-front and honest. "No more lies," I said to myself. "No more hiding. Ever."

As far back as I can remember, I have always known I was homosexual — although I certainly didn't know the word. The earliest sexual arousal I can specifically recollect was in response to a picture of bare-chested TV cowboy star Clint Walker. Later, from about the age of thirteen on, I was as sexually active as opportunity allowed. Those encounters (which lasted through high school) were mostly anonymous "quickies," but, even so, they were the best part of an otherwise unhappy adolescence.

At first I was too excited at being found sexually attractive to really consider the down side of my activities. I did eventually learn the word *homosexual,* along with a good many others: *queer, tearoom, jailbait.* I never felt particularly guilty about my sexuality (except perhaps for the sordid places in which I found partners). I did feel guilty about leading two separate lives, about having to lie and keep secrets.

When I enrolled at American University in Washington, D.C., it meant continuing to live at home in the Maryland suburbs. My relationship with my mother, who raised me by herself, was always difficult at best. By the time I got to college, we had only managed to reach a kind of guarded truce.

Among my complaints about AU, and I had many, was the absence of any gay student group on campus. I eventually found an organization at the University of Maryland, where they had a gay "coffeehouse" on Friday nights. I made up my mind to go.

The group met in a sizable lounge in the cavernous Student Union building. After I finally found the room, I hesitated. There were perhaps thirty people inside, men and women, black and white, not all of them strictly college age. What if they didn't like me? What if I didn't like them? I paced back and forth outside the door for an eternity, then suddenly bolted at top speed into and across the room.

I skidded to a halt next to the refreshment table, stood stiff as a board, and wondered what on earth I was going to do next. Fortunately, a kind man came over to me and said hello. After that, the rest was easy.

Out of those Friday night gatherings came a lot of experience: several short but intense love affairs; other, more-activist meetings; the discovery of gay newspapers and books. All my involvement, however, came to an end when I transferred to Guilford College, a small Quaker school in Greensboro, North Carolina.

In many respects, I was happier at Guilford than I'd ever been in my life: I was enthusiastic about my studies, made lots of new friends, got *involved*. But I was back in the closet. I was at a loss to find the kind of community I'd experienced in D.C.; "gay liberation" had not as yet reached the South.

Once I moved away from home, I seldom went back. Living in Greensboro was cheap, so I stayed and worked during the summers. When I did go back for a visit, I spent most of my time with gay people at group meetings and dances; it was years before I ever went to a gay bar. Living in North Carolina was good for me, mostly: I learned how to make my own way in the world, gained a lot of self-confidence. But I still longed for a gay community like the one I had known.

Finally, in June of 1974, I thought I saw a chance to put the experiences I'd had in D.C. to good use. There was a small, independent paper publishing locally then, called the *Greensboro Sun*. An editorial mentioned the need for "new blood and ideas." So I offered myself and suggested an article, or a series of articles, about gay liberation.

The editor, Rev. Jim Clark, who also headed something called the "Inter-Church Ministry for Social Change," wrote back to me just a few days later:

> I would be very interested in your writing a column for us on an experimental basis. I like your educational approach, for this fits in with our desire to provide the facts for public discussion of the issue.
>
> A little advice: since we are trying to build a broad readership, it is best to tend away from language which might be considered "obscene." While my own feeling is that such words as "war" and "nigger" are obscene, many of those we are trying to reach are easily turned off by any language other than what they thought Nixon used to talk.

I titled my column "On Being Gay," and the first install-
ment ran in the July issue:

> A friend once commented that there was no greater
> anxiety among us than that of homosexuality. The best
> solution to this, I felt and he didn't, was open discussion
> and education. I am now in the process of such an edu-
> cation. I am coming out, and I am learning a great deal.
>
> My friends, wonderfully, have not rejected me, nor
> do they seem to feel sad for me because, I think, they
> can see I am happy with being gay...
>
> This unexpected attitude among my friends re-
> flects, I'm sure, the efforts of those who have struggled
> for sexual freedom these past twenty years, bringing
> this issue to the media, long before I decided to take ad-
> vantage of their struggle. Now I wish to join them.
>
> This space, then, is not simply for my declaration:
> it is to reach you, the gay people of Greensboro. For in
> discovering myself, I have also discovered some things
> about us: that we are not bad, but rather possess a rare
> and valuable quality; that we are not alone, for twenty
> million make quite a crowd even in America; that we
> are not powerless, and many across the country are
> fighting for their rights...

Reverend Clark ran the column with some trepidation and
waited to see what sort of reaction it would provoke. Happily,
my next column was preceded by the following editor's note:

> Last issue we began running this column as an experi-
> ment, requesting reader response. Jim Baxter received
> more mail than any columnist in the history of the *Sun*.
> Thanks.

This historic flood of mail amounted to exactly seven letters — four of them from gay friends I'd coerced into writing. And it included one incredibly confused response, which at the time I thought was too funny to be angry about:

Dear Gay Columnist:

We do understand your dilemma. You are right in wanting open discussion and education on this matter. If I were giving advice to all gays — I would first ask if you have considered seeing your family physician? He will keep this matter confidential. He may know of someone that could be of more help to you. It could be possible that minor surgery would erase your problem. I am sure you are aware of the fact that surgery is now possible that will change a person from one sex to another if that person was born with a defect. If you have a minister by all means see him.

We are all put here on earth for a purpose. Seek and find out what your purpose is in life. I don't know if you believe in God, but if you do you will know God put men on the earth to help multiply and women as his helpmate. If all men were Gays, the earth would cease to exist for man, as there would be no men or women left to populate the world. The Bible has all the answers on this subject, so please try reading it.

Sincerely,
Bea

Little did I realize that more than a decade later there would still be an appalling number of people writing letters very much like that one.

When I wrote, in that first column, that "my friends, wonderfully, have not rejected me," I was exaggerating. I had only told a couple of people, and the process had been tedious. Was I going to have to go through this with everyone? I wondered. Would I always have to phrase the statement ever so carefully, worried that it might be interpreted as a heart-rending confession or an admission of some guilty secret? Would I always have to listen to an equally careful response, one that told me nothing of how my friend really felt?

There had to be a quicker, easier way to get this coming-out business over with! That, I think, was at least part of my motivation to write a newspaper column. For one thing, it was more efficient. I wanted to reach the greatest number of people with the least amount of effort. For another, it was easier to summon the necessary courage. The circumstance of coming out in print made it very easy to avoid direct confrontation, to avoid risking rejection.

My essay for the September issue – the first one all my friends at school would see – was written while I was visiting home in August. While I was there, I also had what was perhaps the most intense one-night stand of my life. It began with dinner and ended – almost twenty-four hours later – with a long, passionate kiss, out in public, on a sidewalk just off Dupont Circle. Back at my mother's apartment, full of passionate fervor, I sat down at the typewriter and pounded out my declaration to Greensboro and North Carolina:

> The fact remains that gays here are not free. Being gay means being free to love all people, of either sex – but until we change the conditioning under which we live, we are free only to *try* to love, against great odds. *There is a new gay world, it is real, it is growing, and it is worth fighting for.* It is a world that offers alternatives, that recognizes that gay means more than the sterile, showy glitter and camp we now associate with the word. Can't you

125

see it? Gay people are no longer servile, harmless, and invisible members of the community, but part of the world as a whole. It *can* happen here. Isn't it worth the risks involved?

The day that issue rolled off the presses, I left dozens of copies lying all over campus, many of them open to my page. And in some cases, slid it under the door of certain individuals' rooms.

For the next couple of weeks I got responses ranging from "You're not *that* Jim Baxter, are you?" to "There *are* two Jim Baxters, aren't there?" After that, people got used to the idea.

I had wanted to be honest with my friends about my sexuality, and had managed to do that. But, even though the September issue of the *Sun* was out all over campus, there was still the matter of telling my mom.

I had long suspected that she had a secret of her own to tell me, just as I had one to tell her. When I was home in August, I said, as I was leaving to come back to Greensboro, "I want you to write me a letter on my twenty-first birthday next month, and I want you to tell me the truth." In honor of my most significant birthday, I thought, my mother and I would be open and honest with each other.

And so we were. She told me I was illegitimate. I told her I was homosexual. It was something of an impasse: neither of us was in a position to call the other names. Her letter to me began:

Dear Jim:

You surprised me with your request for a "Birthday" letter as I expected to tell you. I'm not sure exactly what you want to know but will try to tell you anyhow.

To begin with, your father and I never quite got married. We were supposed to be "engaged" and made some plans, but I guess he really didn't want to be tied down.

When I found I was pregnant, I really didn't know what to do. I visited certain well-known agencies but didn't get much help so made up my own mind to keep the baby. However, I didn't quite know how to handle it afterwards. As a government employee, my record would follow me from job to job — so I couldn't pretend to be married. Also, in those McCarthy times, everyone was investigated for "suitability." The only way I could figure to do it was to lead a double life...

A few days later, I wrote back:

Dear Mom:

Your letter casts a whole different light on a lot of years! I'm very proud of you — really — for both the courage you showed in writing that letter and the courage you've shown in living with me these past twenty-one years. And I thank you — I'm glad you decided to raise me. It took a lot of guts and I realize now how awfully rough it must have been. The news had several effects on me — all of them rather profound but none of them bad. There are a lot of things I'd like to say — how I'd like to apologize for a lot of misjudgments, and how I understand and respect you for keeping the facts to yourself, but mostly I'd like to say thank you. Damn — I've got all kinds of respect for you.

So, turnabout being fair play and all that: if you're going to tell me your big secret, I should be ready to tell you mine. Well, you did and I am, although you may have already put things together for yourself (I wouldn't be surprised!). The news, briefly, is this: as I

come to settle down in the next couple of years, I may
as likely settle down with a man as with a woman. This
is no recent development – homosexual relationships
have been a part of my life for a long, long time ...
None of this is anybody's fault (if you go looking for
blame) – you certainly didn't "fail" me in any respect
and I hope you don't feel that I've failed you. There
are many positive aspects to the world in which "those
people" (of which I am one) live – some are already
present and some are there if you work for them.

I am enclosing copies of a column I write for a community newspaper here. It's a recent development and
part of my efforts to live in one world and not several –
separated by lies and evasions. All of my friends down
here know my story and they still feel the same way
about me – they even threw a smashing birthday party
for me which I'll tell you about some other time.

So, there 'tis. I hope, as I said, that you take the
news well. I feel better for the honesty. Don't you?

Love,
Jim

A few days passed, and then I got a letter back from Mom:

I was glad to get your letter, as I guess I was waiting for
a reaction! You make me sound nobler than I am as it
was probably an essentially selfish action. I guess the
hardest part was having to "live a lie" as I don't lie very
well and don't like to lie at all. It is much better to have
things out in the open, with everyone.

I can't really say your news was a total surprise. I
seem to "know" a lot of things on a psychic level without conscious thought.

My feelings are somewhat mixed on this, as on many subjects, partly because I was brought up in an era when there were no alternatives. I'm sure you know that I am a strong believer in individual rights and freedom. At the same time, I don't really like Gay organizations any more than I like Black militant organizations or Jewish organizations. Although I realize it is necessary to organize to achieve change and fight discrimination, I feel that "exclusiveness" is in the long run stultifying and the individual needs to constantly broaden his horizons.

I also feel that sex – of any kind – is a private thing between two consenting individuals and dislike public displays but then again that may be my upbringing.

I admire your stand, and your effort to find your way. I hope that you can resolve your own conflicts in the ways that are best for you.

As a comment: and not looking to change you, but the "Dear Gay" letter reminded me that I have often thought you might have a hormonal imbalance relating to my own and the shots I took – so if you think such a problem might be a factor a medical check might be in order.

Thanks for telling me – I really appreciate the fact that you have over the years told me many of your feelings and problems as so many people can't talk to their parents at all.

Keep fighting for what you believe in!

Love,

Mom

P.S. As somebody once told me, the truth won't change your real friends and the others don't matter – and it's true!

—————

129

Before I could respond to that remark about "hormones," she sent me another letter with a few additional questions:

> Upon further consideration of your letter, I am still a bit confused. Perhaps if you were willing to answer some questions for me, I would better understand your position.
>
> Are any of your friends that I know gay, or do you have other "circles"? As a college student, have you actually experienced discrimination, etc.? I shouldn't think it would be a significant factor in campus life, particularly if you don't have the effeminate characteristics that people react to. What are the "good points" you spoke of, besides being honest?
>
> Very possibly my questions derive mostly from my own appalling ignorance due to naivete, lack of contact or exposure, and in general, ignorance. As you can imagine, my psychology background only exposed me to the kind of psychiatric junk that we all deplore and which tends to speak in stereotypes.
>
> Anyhow, if you wouldn't mind telling me more about your thoughts and feelings, I would be a better-informed person. Above all, I hope that whatever you choose will result in close and lasting human relationships, which is the most important thing.
>
> Love,
> Mom

By the end of September, my "coming out" was all over. The newspaper column continued for another year. My mom and I began talking to one another as adults, on equal footing, and we both made an effort to put the unhappy past behind us.

♦

There is an epilogue to this story, one that took place just recently. Thirteen years later, I work as editor and publisher of a local gay newspaper. My mother, who retired from her government job, settled in North Carolina.

A rare family reunion was being planned this past spring, and my mother made a strong appeal for me to be there. I'm not very close to my relatives, and I had mixed feelings about spending time with a bunch of people who still called me "Jimmy," and remembered me mostly as a pudgy little cherub.

I also had questions about going through this coming-out business again. Sitting down with her at her kitchen table, I said, "Mom, this reunion means a lot to you. I'd like to know how you'd like me to behave. I'm not saying that I'll do what you ask, but I'd like to know how you feel." She looked puzzled. "How do I respond when they start asking me why I'm not married?"

After an uncomfortable minute of silence, she said, "Well, you don't have to answer. I mean, you could just brush the question off."

I wasn't pleased with that answer, but I thought I'd just let it go. I was still undecided about whether or not to go, when I got a phone call from Mom about two days later.

"Look," she said, "I've been thinking about what we were talking about the other day. I just wanted to tell you that I think you should do whatever you think is right. You tell them exactly what you want to."

That was exactly the answer I'd been hoping for.

Mark Islam

Work in Progress

I was the kid in junior high school that everyone teased mercilessly, the one that absorbed everyone else's loathing. I was the one humiliated at every turn — the last one chosen for teams in the dreaded gym class, the one that opponents *aimed* at when playing dodge ball, the one who elicited suspicion. I knew the agony of having to eat lunch alone in the school cafeteria. I was the class pariah.

I was the class faggot.

Faggot. I was such a naive kid that I didn't even know what the word meant, but it was hurled at me *relentlessly* throughout most of my early adolescence, and I learned the hard way that it was something that non-faggots despised, sometimes violently.

At such a tender age, I couldn't understand what I had done to be so ostracized, so stigmatized, when I knew absolutely *nothing* about sex — hetero-, homo-, or otherwise. So, what did my classmates know that I didn't know? My then-developing mind could only deduce that it must have been something in my behavior that gave me away. Whatever that something was, it was *wrong* in the eyes of the oppressive majority.

But they were right about me. They somehow knew what I didn't know, and didn't have the vocabulary to define. I had same-sex inclinations that I was not mature enough to understand. I am gay, and I spent the rest of my adolescence either trying to understand it, torturing myself over it, or "numbing out" altogether in regards to sex.

By the time I got to high school, I spent most of my time doing the latter: I had become more asexual than anything. While everyone else's hormones were running amok, I was seemingly incapable of thinking of myself in the sexual realm. I didn't date girls because, frankly, I wasn't interested and knew it would be wrong. I didn't do any experimentation with guys, either. Instead, I channeled an enormous amount of energy into my schoolwork, platonic friendships, and plans to leave my provincial hometown.

I came out when I was eighteen. I was a freshman at a school in Boston, and decided to test the waters by coming out to my roommate, who I had an inkling was gay, too. (Even before I was out, my "gaydar" was hard at work, trying to identify others who were like me.) For me, the "coming out" part was not particularly traumatic, but inevitable. In fact, it was a relief to have told someone because then it seemed *real,* not just theoretical. No longer did I have to taunt myself about those issues I was dealing with.

The funny thing about coming out is that once you're out, you are out. You want to tell everyone who ever meant anything to you, even if you're petrified of their reaction. One by one, I was determined to tell everyone I ever considered a friend. I (correctly) figured, that if they rejected me, they were never my friends to begin with. I was lucky. I never lost a friend because of my homosexuality. Indeed, by coming out, I encouraged many of my friends to return the favor by coming out to *me!* Even more surprising, several of my straight friends confessed to having experimented with same-sex encounters.

Coming out, I have learned, is a process. It does not begin and end with just that initial admission of one's gayness; that's just the first among many rungs on the ladder. It's not just the act of telling one's friends and family. That's yet another rung. It's the journey of hacking away at all our protective barriers and defining one's identity in this crazy, often hostile, world.

I'm still doing that. I have no problem admitting that I'm gay because, to me, being gay is not a problem. Homophobia and ignorance are the problems. My tenure as the junior high school outcast taught me that being gay is a problem only *if other people make it a problem!* And then, the way I see it, it isn't even *my* problem; it's theirs. It may sound odd, but I think that being gay has been more of a blessing than a curse. I remember going to a gay pride march in San Francisco and feeling an overwhelming sense of strength, love, and empowerment. When you are gay, you are in no position to discriminate. Instead, you gravitate to other underdogs, which is, in itself, a mind-expanding, humanizing experience. Being gay, then, has enabled me not only to recognize diversity, but to appreciate it. And that's precisely why I'm proud to be gay.

My next step in the coming-out process is coming to terms with my gay *sexuality,* which will be a harder nut to crack, so to speak.

While I have few problems with my gay identity (the "homo" part of "homosexual"), I definitely have an undeveloped sense not just of gay sexuality, but of sexuality in general. On an intellectual level, I can accept myself as a gay man; it's really no problem. On a sexual level, I have a more difficult time. I am intimidated by sex. I've never been comfortable in the role of the sexual aggressor. Perhaps it stems from my fears of rejection and other self-esteem issues, particularly issues about my body and appearance. Every time I sense that someone is attracted to me, I run in the other direction. I always find it ironic that straights stereotype gay men as being promiscuous, because I have been celibate for two years. (Where *does* the time go?)

The thing is, just because you aren't "doing it" doesn't mean you aren't "it."

My longest-running relationship, where sex was involved, lasted for about three months. I met him in Hollywood and felt an instant magnetism, like an awakening of sorts. I was turned on for the first time in a long time. I was not scared of the feeling at all, but, instead, felt an enormous adrenaline-like rush. We slept together on the second date, and, as I recall, it was nice — warm, playful, affectionate, wet. Still, no matter how much he tried to reassure me, I was never able to relax enough to really enjoy it. Most of my previous sexual experiences, with both men *and* women, produced the same kind of anxiety.

I try to tell myself that I haven't had sex in so long because I've been so actively pursuing my career. That's only partially true. My career *does* absorb most of my time and energy. Still, lots of people are able to juggle careers and relationships. If I am honest with myself, I'd have to say that I'm just intimidated/frightened/threatened by issues of sexuality. I recently saw someone on "Oprah" who said something to the effect that, "Our fear is the beacon to the truth." She is right. By confronting that thing that makes me fearful, I am leading myself to the truth. There is a reason that I am threatened by sex; so, I've made myself asexual to avoid dealing with that bigger, potentially paralyzing issue. In doing so, I have created blocks that surface in other areas of my life — feelings of hopelessness, anxiety, depression — which is precisely why I must confront my asexuality. I am beginning to understand that I can never get over these issues unless I am willing to take risks and just experiment, even if it involves failure and humiliation. This is my next hurdle.

I've been joking that 1993 is either the year I get rich or the year I get laid. As I'm writing this, the year is nearly half over, and neither has happened yet. But I am ever hopeful. The truth is, I really would like to have sex with someone again. Not just for the sake of sex itself, but for the closeness and intimacy that all human beings need. I often think to myself, "If I were to die by the end of the day, would I have done everything I wanted to do?" For me, it's a sobering thought, because I am so fearless in nearly every other area of my life. I can honestly say that I have very few regrets, but the main regret is my unhealthy avoidance of sex. However, if I know one thing about life it is this: we do things at our own time and at our own pace. That's why some men don't come out until they've been married for twenty years − they just weren't ready. I'm feeling like I'm now finally ready to tackle my issues about sexuality and − dare I say it?? − *erotophobia*.

Laurence Wolf

Is It Ever Too Late?

Ve get too soon oldt undt too late schmart.

I have no reason to doubt that old Pennsylvania Dutch saying, and I've doubted plenty of things in my day. Today, I'm learning that a man can love me. All the reward I need from him is the smile on his face, the joy in his eyes, and the sincerity in his voice as he tells me that he is happy I've come into his life. Just in the nick of time, you might say: we recently celebrated his seventieth and my sixty-fifth birthdays.

◆

When did I first know I was different? I was a "lefty" among right-handers in grade school. I was almost the only bookworm in the crowd. I was ill more often than the other children, and I gave a lot of thought to avoiding the neighborhood bullies. I was different. So, when the rest of the guys suddenly became interested in girls and I didn't, it was like everything else in my life — they went one way and I went another.

My first same-sex experience was in junior high. Herbie liked me to stroke his penis, so we'd sneak up to the roof and make sure no one else was there. It was flat, with chimney stacks and stairway kiosks to hide behind. He never returned the favor, which annoyed me. Then Herbie moved away, and there were no other Herbies, though I looked sharply for any sign of this "difference" among my small group of pals. No "older man" came along, either.

My energy went into a helluva lot of reading — novels, history, biography, and, later on, politics. No one ever told me I was a faggot, so I just buried my sexuality deep inside. Any mention of sex was Absolutely Forbidden in our household, and my parents never showed any physical affection for each other. By the time I was in my teens, they were arguing constantly, and although sexual topics entered into that, they used figures of speech to disguise them. By the time I'd taken a college course in psychology, I decided that I was a case of arrested development as far as sex was concerned. It was a popular theory at the time, and seemed to be a handy explanation.

My college years ended early, because I was drafted to fight in the army during World War II. On a troop train one night, the guy sharing my bunk fucked me. That was a nice new experience. I didn't say a word — sex was, after all, unspeakable — and he never brought it up again. After basic training, overnight passes became available. I found a bar full of men interested in other men, but I rarely went there because of my fear that someone from my battalion might show up. I had all I could handle just surviving the emotional strain of army wartime regimentation.

I eventually went overseas just in time for the end of the war in the Pacific, narrowly missing combat duty. During that time, my life resumed its usual sexlessness.

It took me a long time to recall what I had actually done those few nights when I had bunked with another guy in town. I finally remembered, dimly: I was the bottom. How did the other guy know what I wanted? How did we meet at the bar? Those memories are still repressed. At any rate, it was while I was in the army that I decided I should try to pursue the opposite sex.

When I tried to figure out what sort of woman I wanted, I came up with a list of characteristics that were utterly unrealistic. I had already lived so much of my life alone, I just reconciled myself to living the rest of it alone too. I buried myself in my work.

After the war I went to graduate school. My roommate introduced me to a blonde, petite, attractive young woman. We fell in love, married, and went off to my first professional employment together. My Terrible Problem was finally solved! Children came along, and with them a house in the suburbs, and then a finer house in town. When our youngest was in high school, my wife said she'd had enough of a husband who spent entirely too much time at his books. The divorce was amicable.

I owe my coming out to my closest friend. I'd known Bob for decades, as a friend and professional colleague. I had never had the slightest clue that he was gay. Then, one day, he dropped by my house and started to tell me that he was a queer, that psychiatric counseling had been no help, that he could no longer tolerate his internal conflicts, and that his wife and some of his children could not accept his gayness. I found myself interrupting him. I admitted, in almost a whisper, that I too was "sexually ambiguous."

When he left, I was in a daze. Honesty with my closest pal had made me voice, for the first time in my life, my most deeply hidden secret. From then on, I had not just a friend and colleague, but an elder brother. With his encouragement I went to the local gay bars with him and his lover. And although it was several years before I could go alone, I found I could dance there. I could never dance with a woman; there was always too much uncontrollable tension. Bob got me to join several gay organizations, and since functioning on committees comes naturally to me, this was a good way to become active in the gay scene.

After I came out, all the usual stereotypes I had about gay men crashed, one after another. I found I was walking with a quicker step and felt twenty years younger. I was euphoric whenever I entered a gay environment or felt the electric thrill of dancing in the midst of a mob of moving men. Euphoria was knowing in my heart that being gay was all right.

Frustration soon replaced euphoria, however — frustration at wanting someone to share my life with, someone with whom I could have intimate rapport, someone with whom to consummate my liberation, and not finding him. Everyone seemed to be looking for someone younger, giving me that "Oh, I can't see you because you're over thirty" look. I thought that gay guys of my vintage were snugly in their closets where I'd never find them.

There was rage, too, surfacing as the years of frustration went by: rage at a society that preached equality and practiced bigotry, and rage at a gay community that segregated itself. I got a constriction in my gut when I read ads that specified, "No fems!" or that meant someone less than half my age when an "older man" was sought. I found that most gay men were much too conservative for me. Where was the flamboyance, the defiant alienation, the individuality and creativity that gays were supposed to have?

It was about six years after my coming out that I met Jerry, my lover — six sexless years of newfound inner strength, of seeing the world in new ways, and of disillusionment and heartache. Bob had written a letter that was published in a local gay paper, to which Jerry replied. Knowing my painful loneliness, Bob passed Jerry's name and address to me, and a lively correspondence developed. We were both busy people, and it was several months before we met, but we began to "click" right away. I found acceptance, affection, intimacy, and the same wacky sense of humor that I have. I have found that my love muscle can be delightfully hard for longer than I ever thought possible; that the whole body is sensually sensational.

If only I'd known this fifty years ago!

Don Sakers

Stone Walls

It was five years after Stonewall, and I was a junior in high school.

Half a decade before, over four hundred gays had taken to the streets to protest the closing of the Stonewall Inn. How aptly gay rights activists named that brief protest in the Greenwich Village summer of 1969: the Stonewall Riot. For it was like the smashing of a great stone wall across society, a bulwark of fear and prejudice, built to keep gays out. With Stonewall, the barriers were torn down and a new world arose.

As I came into adolescence, homosexuality was no longer "the love that dared not speak its name." Nor was it, as one commentator quipped, "the neurosis that would not shut up." The gay rights movement had done this: homosexuality could no longer be ignored; it could not be hushed up. The word *gay* was a permanent part of America's social consciousness. Whatever the others would do to us, they could never again pretend that we didn't exist.

Five years after Stonewall. The reds and oranges of autumn spread across central Maryland, and in my suburban Baltimore high school, classes were just beginning. Stonewall had torn down the major barriers in society, but I would still have my own stone walls to smash ... or batter my head against.

The first was easy: recognizing that I could be attracted to other guys. The world of 1974 had prepared me for the concept; the books I read (mostly science fiction) led me to believe that most human beings were fundamentally ambisexual. By junior year, I was ready to admit to myself that there were boys I found attractive ... and to take another little step toward the truth, by writing in my journal that "so far" there were no girls that attracted me.

I was on a collision course with the second stone wall. So far, I had just a teenager's unfocused sexuality; I still had not admitted to myself that I was exclusively gay.

The impetus to carry me over that barrier showed up quickly. My life changed that autumn. I had always been the outcast — I was bright, I read science fiction, I was no good at softball or basketball. I was prepared to remain an outcast forever ... until I met a handful of others who were also outcasts. A dozen of us banded together and turned mutual loneliness into a unity that lasted far beyond our high school years.

It was a time of change, a time of possibilities, as we all learned to lower our defenses and open ourselves to one another. And in the course of this learning, something marvelous and terrible happened: I fell in love.

Fred was perhaps an unlikely choice for a first love — gangly, manic, highly intelligent yet very insecure. As I look at yearbook pictures and remember those days, I find it hard to believe that any of us were attractive, with our long, unkempt hair and our hysterical juvenile behavior. Yet we were all in the same condition; if now I can see through Fred's arrogant posturing, I can also understand the vulnerability and loneliness in which I saw a kindred soul.

Admitting that I was in love with Fred was easy. The rest wasn't — because I'd made the oldest mistake in the book. I'd lost my heart to a straight boy.

The first person I told was my best friend Ann. Her response was everything I could have wished for: supportive, accepting, and compassionate. During the next few months, as I worked through the difficult process of dealing with my first romantic interest, Ann was my sole confidant.

With the melodramatic instincts of teenagers, we at once decided that Fred must never know of my attraction to him. He might begin to wonder, we decided, if he had done something to encourage me ... and while I was strong enough to face the fact of being gay, we had no such illusions about Fred's strength.

For months I struggled with my developing feelings. Once or twice, late-night parties turned into romantic sessions as boys and girls paired off to different corners of the basement for adolescent kissing and petting; I would sit quietly on the couch, watching Fred and his current girlfriend, and hold back tears of self-pity. Where she was, I wanted to be.

Eventually I was able to face reality and give up chasing Fred. By then, I was attracted to other boys and had enough to keep me busy without pining.

The happy ending to this story is that a year or so later, I did tell Fred. He was flattered, although uninterested. Now, a decade later, Fred and I are still close friends.

As I dealt with my feelings for Fred, both Ann and I met the next, and most serious, stone wall: ignorance. Neither of us had ever met a gay person, and our society provided us with few role models to show how gays were supposed to behave. I knew I wasn't a "sissy," and I knew that I didn't harbor a secret desire to be a woman. Beyond that, I knew nothing. Like so many gays before and since, I crept along in the darkness, alone. I was certain no one had ever experienced the feelings I was experiencing. Certainly no one had ever said anything about it.

Two things came together to build a bridge over that barricade of ignorance and loneliness: books and current events.

It was the books that first provided me with good gay role models. Patricia Nell Warren's *The Front Runner* electrified me, ended my solitude, and gave me words for those feelings that I thought no one had ever shared. Mary Renault's *Fire from Heaven* and *The Persian Boy* told me what love between men could be at its best. Assorted short stories gave me glimpses of the strange, frightening, and yet intriguing gay world. And Laura Z. Hobson's *Consenting Adult* was true ambrosia, nourishment for the spirit.

Then, as I started my senior year, Leonard Matlovich sued the U.S. Air Force. Matlovich, a decorated war hero, had been discharged because he wrote a letter to his commanding officer stating that he was gay. And then, amazingly, he dared to fight the Air Force across the front pages of the nation. In one fell swoop, Ann and I discovered gay activism and encountered the thrilling concept that one could be strong, gay, and proud.

In the meantime, another stone wall stood before me, one that I would not succeed in passing for another decade. My father, snooping as many parents do, came across my private journal and read enough to realize the Awful Truth. After several angry and emotional confrontations, we made an unspoken agreement to ignore the matter. And ignore it we did. For the next few years, family dinners were perfectly cordial and civilized, but the entire concept of homosexuality sat unregarded in the middle of the table, right between the mashed potatoes and the peas. Only much later, after many storms and tears and much growing up on both sides, did my parents and I ultimately make peace.

But that was for the future. By the end of that wonderful and terrible year of 1975, I had emerged from darkness and ignorance into the bright light of full self-knowledge and pride. And Ann had accompanied me every step of the way. In my journal I could truthfully refer to myself as "young and beautiful and gay and proud."

The next barrier in my development was, in many ways, the most difficult one. Although I had been in love, I had not yet made love. I started college as a virgin, and remained that way through my entire freshman year.

It wasn't, in fact, until the summer of 1977 that I was to find my first lover and give up that unwanted virginity.

I met Bill at a birthday party for a mutual friend. Fred and the others were well adjusted to my gayness, and they (and I) made no great secret of my sexual orientation. Bill kept quiet at the party, but called me the next day and we made a date. We spent a lazy summer afternoon rowing in the harbor, exploring downtown Baltimore, and talking.

It wasn't until later, as I heard stories of other guys' first sexual encounters, that I came to appreciate how lucky I was with Bill. He was compassionate, gentle, and very concerned with my feelings. He had suffered much guilt his first time, and he wanted to spare me that ordeal. As a result, it took me four days to convince him that I truly wanted him to go to bed with me.

That first experience, and the ones that followed, could not have been better. My parents were away at a baseball game; with Prokofiev and Wagner on the stereo, we made slow, gentle love together. Afterward we cuddled, showered, and

146

left the house just as the last pitch of the baseball game was called on the radio.

Because of Bill's caring and his willingness to help ("If you'd rather be alone now, you can take me home; I'll understand," he offered), I suffered none of the guilt and anguish that many of my friends felt their first time.

Our relationship as lovers lasted three months. Despite some mutual friends and some of the same interests, we didn't have that much in common. We both knew that it was time to end it and move on to something else. Bill, compassionate as ever, let me down as gently as possible. For a year or so after, we stayed in contact and saw one another fairly often; then he moved away and my first love affair was completely done. Sometimes I feel left out, when discussion turns to the angst and pain of first love – but on the whole, I am happier that I had the good fortune to find someone like Bill.

There were still walls ahead – contacts with the gay world; the challenge of a mature, ongoing relationship between two adults; coming out dramatically and publicly as the author of a gay teenage romance novel – but the real struggle was over, for I had accepted myself. I now had an identity as a gay person.

A succession of stone walls ... but these walls were not merely barriers to progress. Rather, they were like the stone walls at various levels of a terraced garden – and each wall passed took me further, lifted me higher, and revealed to me the splendors of yet another section of the garden. Looking back, some of the walls that took great effort to cross seem easy, and some scarcely seem like walls at all. Ahead there will be more walls, more effort, and gardens far more splendid than any that have come before.

Edward Powell

Zola*

I dressed up for the first time during Halloween, like every gay man does. I was the night manager of the Bostonian Market on Tremont Street in Boston, and my boss asked me to come to work in drag. He knew at the time I was working with makeup for a modeling agency in Brookline. I had been out for years by then. I've been gay since I was eleven. I was never a repressed homosexual.

He asked me to come in drag, so I did, and I looked pretty good. I had on this feather boa, a fuchsia silk dress, and a pillbox hat. Snakeskin pumps. And I started coming around to Jacques, a local drag bar, more often. One of the performers at that time, Tony Rochester, told me that I could look like Grace Jones. I started doing Grace Jones, and it just evolved out of that. I've been doing drag since 1988, so it's been six years.

I'm from a small town called Groton, Massachusetts. I was the only black kid in my school. I didn't know what gay was. This guy who lived up the hill from us, Stephan, introduced me to the whole thing in my kitchen, where I performed oral sex on him. I had a little trouble with it at first. I thought it was wrong, but it felt right.

* Based on an interview with Adrien Saks conducted November 9, 1993.

148

I was never really a hit with women anyway, although I always wanted a girlfriend. I did have one when I was twelve or thirteen. Brandy and I used to make out underneath the stairs at the school.

There wasn't really a gay scene in Groton. There was just Stephan. He was the only person I had sex with. Then we moved to Ayer, and there's an army base called Fort Devens nearby. I went to Fort Devens sometimes to meet soldiers. There was a bookstore in Ayer that had a gay section. It had all the gay magazines on the bottom. That was my first introduction to *Gay Community News* and their personals section.

I really came out when I went into the air force. I was in for two years, and then I was kicked out because I am gay. My boss actually cried when I left. She was all upset, and she didn't want me to go. Anything I've ever done in my life, I've excelled in. I am very driven. The air force was no exception, and I was a good airman.

I loved the air force. It was really good for me. I wanted to go into the air force since I was thirteen. I was very happy about having that goal and then making it happen. It was a very strange experience for me, though. It was the first time I had ever been away from my house and my parents. They were extremely overprotective, and I didn't get much of a chance to do the things that I wanted to do when I was younger.

There are a lot of gay people in the military. A lot. It was a whole little network, so we all knew when a new child came on to the base. That's what we called them, the children. We had a lot of straight friends who knew us and liked us, too. It was a lot of fun. We partied together. Oh, god, did we party. It was a good time in my life, going to Mississippi, Texas, and eventually New Mexico. That's where I was discharged. I was

149

stationed in Cannon Air Force Base in Clovis, New Mexico. It's a very small, awful town.

I did have a couple of experiences on the base, but I could count them on one hand. I did it off base. That way no one would know my business. I was going out with this guy named Curtis. I was seeing him for a while and I contracted syphilis from him. It was my first venereal disease, and of course, I was scared half to death. Things were happening to my body, and I didn't know what to do. Instead of going to a private doctor, I went to the air force doctor on the base. He told me what it was, and he treated me. Because of where I had contracted the disease, though, he had to go to higher authorities and report it. It was mandatory that he did that, and once he reported it, the wheels of supposed justice took their course. I was discharged.

I wonder what I would be doing now if I had stayed in for my full term. I would probably be doing something totally different, not female impersonation. At that time I had no desire to do this; I didn't want to entertain. This never would have happened if they hadn't discharged me. The United States Air Force made me a woman!

You definitely get treated differently when you start out as a guy and then you come onto the scene as a queen. When I first started coming out I was a boy, of course, and people had one perception of me. When I started doing drag, people treated me differently. The queens who thought I was cute as a guy didn't exactly lose respect for me, but they had a different perception of me. They thought I was competition or I wanted to become a woman. They didn't think about or remember the way I had acted in the past, before doing drag.

Guys who thought I was cute tended not to want to be bothered, because they didn't like drag queens. I didn't let that bother me, though. I couldn't let it. This is what I wanted to do.

As far as meeting men, I don't usually. I have two situations. When guys who are attracted to me as Edward find out that I do shows, they're not really thrilled about it. The problem is that they see me as a drag queen. I see myself as a female impersonator. I am a man who dresses up as a woman to entertain. That's what I am. And I think it would be a different story if they saw me as a professional. That's the whole idea. I am a professional entertainer.

Guys who meet me as Zola are caught up in the whole Zola thing, the glamour and the fact that I look like a woman. I talk a little softer and my mannerisms are a little bit more feminine. They tend to just want to deal with that, and they don't want to deal with the fact that I am a man. So I don't meet men often. Plus, I work too much. Every night I'm doing something. So, I don't get a chance to meet men socially. I don't get a chance to go to parties very often and just hang out with guys. And when I do, if somebody asks somebody else about me, they don't say, "That's Edward." They say, "That's Zola. She's a drag queen. You should see her show." And men are put off by that.

I am a professional female impersonator. I present my idea of womanhood, and I also impersonate actual people. I impersonate Grace Jones, Whitney Houston, Sade, and RuPaul. By next week I'll have Janet Jackson and Angela Bassett as Tina Turner. And I do a little bit of comedy. I'm also the show director here at Jacques Cabaret. We do shows seven nights a week, and I'm in charge of every show. I make the schedule up, I pay the entertainers, and I conduct staff meetings to talk about the shows and their quality. Basically, I am paid to be bitchy.

It's nice to get dressed. I like wearing nice clothes and jewelry. I like being well-put together. When I am done with it, though, I've got this timer that clicks on. During the course of the night my timer is winding down and when it gets to be a certain hour I just want to get out of this stuff. I just want to take it off. Usually when I go home, I hit the door and my wig goes off, my lashes go off, the shoes go off, the hose go off, the bra goes off, and the tits go flying. It's just such a relief. And finally when you can reach down there and grab your dick out of the position that it's in and just let it hang! I can't describe the relief. It's just great.

I have no desire to be a woman. Just no desire. I am a lazy person, basically, and to be a woman is a lot of work — to be the type of woman that I would want to be. I think women have so many advantages as to their looks and how they can change them. How their image can be changed. Just the way they dress, what they put on, how their makeup is applied. They have such control. To be a woman I would always want to be glamorous. Because I think that's the best way to look. I'm not saying that you always have to wear evening gowns, twenty-four hours a day. I'm not talking about that. You can look glamorous and well put-together without having to go through such things.

I feel it's very important that you like your work. I just don't understand people who go to work and can't stand their job. I couldn't see it. Not every job, of course, can be fun. If you're a ditch digger, it's not going to be that much fun. If that's what you want to do, do it, but if you're tired of being a ditch digger, then stop digging ditches. Of course, in certain situations it's easier said than done. But at least try instead of complaining.

I love pageants. They're fun. I used to be very bitchy during them. Very bitchy, and really irritable. Now, I've calmed down a little. I've relaxed. My titles are Miss Jacques,

Miss DeRocco's, Miss Boston, Miss Massachusetts, Miss Gay New England, Miss North Shore. I've entered the Miss Massachusetts, U.S.A., Pageant twice and I've gotten second runner-up twice. It bothers me that I haven't won. It's my fault, though, and I've learned what to do to win next time.

You see pageants are very important to me. I'm not competitive in everyday life. I don't believe in that. But when it's a structured competition, then I'm very competitive. Pageants are important because they help you grow. Every pageant I've done let me evolve into a better entertainer. When you are in a bar that has a show seven nights a week, and you work six of them, you have to grow. You can't get stale and old. That's when people don't come to see your show or they start talking bad about you. I can take all the good stuff you want to talk, but when people start talking bad about me, I don't like that. So I try to do my best to get new costumes or rotate costumes so that people don't see the same old thing all the time. I try to rotate my music around, and I get inspired to do some new stuff.

My last new character was Sade. And Sade didn't go off too well the first time I did it. So I kind of abandoned her. I had to rethink her. I brought it out again and people like it much better now. That's the first time that's ever happened. So now I'm going to be doing Angela Bassett as Tina Turner, which will be a strange one to do. I'll be doing someone doing somebody.

RuPaul is only by popular demand, because people asked me to do it. I really didn't want to. I thought it was very redundant. A female impersonator doing a female impersonator. I thought that was kind of stupid. Everybody asked me to do it, though, and she's a very popular character.

In a few weeks I'll be giving up my crown as Miss Gay New England. I'll have six dancers, including myself as Janet Jackson, and it'll be just like the video. Three girls and three guys. I think that's the most people that have ever been on the Jacques stage at one time. I'm very excited about it. And I'll be doing Ike and Tina Turner. Kevin will be Ike.

I'm giving up this title, I'm not even entering the pageant, and I've already spent sixty dollars for the choker to be made. Just the dance outfit for the first number will probably cost fifty dollars, but that's because my friend, Norell, is making it. It would be more if someone else was. The wig is about fifty. For the second number, the other wig will be another fifty dollars. It will be seventy dollars just for the beads to rebead the outfit. The gown will probably cost three hundred dollars. Flowers — thirty dollars. I'll borrow the shoes, but I have to get bones for the Janet Jackson outfit. Seven hundred and twenty dollars total. I'll have six dancers, too, and I'll probably have to buy a drink for each of them. That's what you go through.

It's a shame that a lot of club owners don't realize how much money goes into performing. They have no idea. No clue that I'm spending seven hundred and twenty dollars. If they had any idea how much I spend, and the time and the effort that I put into it, they wouldn't so freely hand you fifty dollars and think that they're doing you a great favor. They're not. But that's the problem that Boston has. People here don't realize the effort and the things you have to do.

Partly what makes it worth it is that I'll have all this stuff. Not only will I use it here, but when I do shows all across New England. When I sell myself to prospective clubs, I always say my costumes and makeup cost money. I do have good stuff, and I do spend money. What really makes it worth it is personal satisfaction. When I step out on stage, do a number, and hear the applause. People scream and carry on. That makes it worth it. It sounds corny but it's true. That's what I like. I have a reputation. When people hear the name Zola, they say, "Oh, I've seen her show at such and such a place. She's good." I've heard that. When people hear my name, when I'm coming out on stage, they pay attention. They turn around.

All of a sudden, drag is very fashionable. At least that makes it easier. There are still people who can't get used to the idea of drag queens, but sometimes you can change their minds if they see your show and see that you're serious about it. Some of them you just can't sway. You have to just go right on by them.

I'm very happy that for the first time we have a positive influence in the drag world with RuPaul. She's doesn't look like the stereotype of a drag queen. When people think of drag they think of that very funny drag, like Tootsie and Uncle Miltie. Not that many people know about the glamour and beauty. They think of comedy. A lot of television shows have these very straight guys putting on dresses. It's making a comedy out of it. You see this big old black guy dressed as his grandmama playing basketball. Give me a break.

I believe the most important thing is that you have to love yourself. You can't love anybody else or have respect for anybody else if you don't love and respect yourself. If you are coming out, you have to find yourself and learn more about yourself before you can start doing anything. If you're coming out and doing female impersonation, establish your true friends and hold on to them, because everyone else that you meet will be very transient. There are very few friends that you'll meet along the way that will actually stick with you all the way. There can be a lot of shade, but fortunately there's not so much in Boston. There's a family atmosphere here. We all help each other out, and we all go to see each others' shows. We all have a good time together, and it's real.

M. Scott Mallinger

Lives & Lies in South Jersey

Now that my former classmates are going away to college, I am finally able to see them for what they are: pompous, judgmental, and hypocritical asses. My idealistic vision of who and what my friends are has given way to a more cynical, and sadly, to a more realistic perception. They like a person not for who he is, but rather for what they think he represents. Knowing that I am gay, and yet pretending to be straight, what did I actually represent? I think I finally know.

As a result of dealing with my sexual orientation I have gained insight and self-understanding. There's truth in the Bible's words "In wisdom, there is much grief: and he that increaseth knowledge increaseth sorrow." My youthful aspirations of having a thousand friends, going to an Ivy League school, and having 2.2 kids and a white picket fence have dissipated into nothingness; and I'm not sure the emptiness that's left can ever be totally filled.

This past April 12, I celebrated my eighteenth birthday alone. I choose to remain detached from my peers, because I would rather be lonely than lie to people about who I am. I believe lying to create an image for oneself is a reflection of shame, and I am not ashamed of who I am. Discreet, yes, but not ashamed.

Although I've wanted to come out for a few years, I have always remained trapped in the closet due to my fear of others' hostility toward my family and myself. But I would like to explain what it has been like to grow up trapped in this stifling space, repressed to the point that I was unable to grow as a person. Forced to remain silent while peers, classmates, and even friends unknowingly damned me.

Ever since elementary school, the name "faggot" has always been associated with something ugly, corrupt, and perverse. To be called a faggot was the ultimate insult that any seven- or eight-year-old could throw at you. Ten years later the same rule holds true.

I think I was in second grade when I heard the word *faggot* for the first time. It had no special meaning for me. I had been taught by my folks about this thing called homosexuality, about men loving men, long before school. And although my parents weren't as phobic as the children, they too were against this thing which seemed to me just as natural as any other kind of loving. To my prepubescent mind, loving was the most natural thing a person could do.

Today I appear like the stereotypical heterosexual, but as a child I would frequently play with the girls. I would prefer to trade stickers and play hopscotch with them than be athletic with the boys. I giggled and squealed, and despite the fact that I didn't play dress-up, my gestures were undeniably feminine. My parents looked on in fear, while at the same time hating themselves for suspecting what their son was to become.

I was shamed into lowering my voice, training myself not to laugh in such a high pitch, or not to laugh at all. I tried to always remain calm and collected; I had to remain in constant control of who I appeared to be, so that who I really was wouldn't peek through. After a while, I became quite good at it. I lied to my parents, friends, and even to myself. At the price of appearing straight, I lost my childhood.

Because of my present appearance, and a reputation for being with older women, no one has ever doubted my masculinity. But I find it incredibly fascinating, and sometimes horrifying, to hear friends and co-workers talk about gays. On any other topic they are fine, and we can discuss rationally their feelings. Death, abortion, God ... but mention the word *gay*, and they tighten up inside and cringe. Some will wave their arms about, or let their hands dangle from their wrists, and call themselves "funny boys," or "homos." But when they do that, they're not just making fun. They are not playing. They are hating.

"I bet that new guy in the deli is one of those faggots," one cashier told me when I was working at a local supermarket. My stomach sank. I wished she wouldn't say anything more...

"Weirdo. They should all be killed, as far as I'm concerned." I looked down into her sweet, innocent face. This girl wouldn't hurt a fly. She seemed to be as pure as the Madonna Herself. Then to say something like that? It wasn't her talking; it was religion, and society. She had been brainwashed. If someone like this girl could be taught such hatred, then no one was safe. I asked her if she thought he still deserved a job with us. "Faggots," she complained. "Why don't they just stay in Gatsby's?"

Kids as far down as first grade know that Gatsby's is a gay bar. It is where the dirty old faggots hang out. No, the children don't even know what a faggot is yet, but they know it's not good.

Socialization took its toll on me as well. Consciously I always defended homosexuals, perhaps knowing deep down that I was one, but after a while, I also began believing what all the kids had said. I didn't realize this until fairly recently, when I first attempted to get into Gatsby's. I made it as far as the parking lot, got out of my car, and stood there, paralyzed with fear.

As the cool air blew past my face, I saw nice-looking people walking past me, going in and out of the bar. But they weren't just nice-looking people to me. They were demons from my childhood, monsters from my closeted past, and they terrified me. What was I doing in this place? I was not only confronting them, I was joining them!

I walked up to the door, felt sick to my stomach, and returned to my car. After recovering for ten or fifteen minutes, I got up again. For the second time, I stood motionless for what seemed an eternity, then approached the door, only to grow sick again. Finally, two hours later, I went home, never actually getting through the door.

Homophobia seems to have always been around, and was in fact encouraged, if not by the staff, by the literature that the Cherry Hill school system taught. Salinger's classic *Catcher in the Rye* is just one fine example of this fear and paranoia surrounding men loving men. Holden Caufield, the protagonist, feared any signs of affection one man might give to another. A pat on the leg, being stroked on the head ... Holden was more afraid that he might be gay than others, and he used this fear to alienate himself.

Class discussions could be even more negative, like my eleventh-grade English class's discussion of Walt Whitman's *Leaves of Grass*. In the short biography of the poet printed in the anthology there was a line that said Whitman had an "unusual attraction towards other men."

Naturally this intrigued the students, who preferred to crack offensive AIDS jokes and read perversity between the textual lines. Some students were outraged that they had to read homosexual poetry, declaring that faggots were killing the world with AIDS and that they should all be rounded up and shot. Meanwhile I could only sit back, nodding or shaking my head, pretending that I could understand what everyone else was going through. But how could I, when I knew everything they said was wrong?

Guilt surged within me; how could I just sit back and condemn myself and those like me to this kind of hysteria? Wasn't I a hypocrite by virtue of my silence? How could I curse World War II Germany for sitting idly by and allowing the Jews to be slaughtered when in fact I was allowing the same thing to happen now, if not literally, then at least on an emotional level?

I shamed myself as I realized that I was too afraid of being associated with homosexuals, that I could not defend myself for fear that someone might find out who I really was. I had begun to buy into this deal that if I was gay, I couldn't be a functioning, stable member of society.

What should have been a forty-two-minute discussion of Whitman's poetry wound up being a sermon by the teacher that alternative lifestyles were a fact of life, and that they were just as acceptable as straight relationships. This brought about as much laughter as it did disbelief. I knew I had to do something.

I decided that I wanted to get connected in some way to the gay community – to find my niche and to fill the void that had pervaded my soul ever since I discovered I wasn't the Stepford Child I was raised to be. To my utter shock, I learned that "South Jersey gay life" didn't exist. With the exception of the one infamous gay bar, there was no such thing as gay life in South Jersey.

I crusaded with the support of some of my high school faculty to get a gay support group together. I talked to counselors; I wrote letters. I felt that silence was ignorance, and that ignorance was hatred. If nothing else, I wanted one or two gay books in the school library. I felt that this would be a first step toward public acceptance. But my appeal to the school librarian had no effect. Allowing homosexual literature into the school library would be admitting that there are homosexuals not just in Gatsby's, but in the real world — on the streets, in the boardrooms, in the classrooms, and in the locker rooms. The board of education wouldn't tolerate it.

I was furious: they were pushing me aside like a second-class citizen, as if gay people didn't count, as if our feelings were unimportant. The more I wrote, or even thought about my predicament, the angrier I got. I would never become a second-class citizen.

I began to write essays on homosexuality, and then finally a short story for the school's highly acclaimed literary magazine. At this point I would have been willing to put a name on my writing, but several people counseled against it. Sent in anonymously, my piece told the first-person story of a guy realizing for the first time that he was gay. He was somewhat relieved that he was not alone, but more overwhelming was the disgrace and pain he experienced.

I gave the story to a guidance counselor who gave it to the man in charge of the magazine. It came back to me, approved. I was permitted to submit it to the literary group, but it had to have a name on it. With a little help, I chose the name Harvey Milk.

The story was reviewed by a group of students. Midway through reading the piece one girl shrieked, "I think this guy's a faggot." Brilliant deduction, I thought silently. When they were through reading the story, the students tried desperately to figure out who wrote the piece. They questioned different phrases and practically made a list of possible candidates.

Images of students walking down the hall with scarlet H's on their Izod shirts filled my mind. I shuddered. "Does it really matter who wrote it?" I asked. They all looked up, embarrassed, and shook their heads. They knew the author didn't want to be known. They just didn't know why.

I had agreed to hand it in anonymously because I didn't want gayness to have a face or a look. I wanted anyone to be a possible homosexual. Then finally we'd all be equal. It worked.

Unfortunately, my piece was then submitted to the principal. It was rejected. My story would remain unpublished. I was disappointed but not exactly shocked. How could I expect to get attention or respect in a town that lives on illusions and lies, from people who pretend to be what they aren't and to have what they don't? A little bit of honesty horrifies a society of liars.

The members of the literary group began to pass around a petition, and many of the teachers whom I'd known for years read my piece, called "The Day Superman Died." As far as I know, everyone was for its publication. I don't pretend that it was a great literary treasure, but I do think it is an important issue. Obviously a lot of other people did too. Alas, the taxpayers had the last say.

The only acknowledgment my piece received were two pages dedicated to the dead-superhero theme which included in small print the words "literary piece censored." It was a sickening mockery of what I had hoped could help bridge the gap between homophobic hatred and understanding.

At this point I had tired of South Jersey and decided to search for a place I could belong. Finally, I turned to Philadelphia.

With the help of my guidance counselor, I got a list of numbers to call. With each touch of the push-button phone, my heart leaped and my stomach churned. I would be confessing the secrets of my sexuality to total strangers, not even knowing who they were or if they really cared.

To make matters worse, rarely did any person answer the phone. I usually received a recorded message. Always feeling like an idiot, but responding to the machine nonetheless, I would state my name and what I wanted. However, when my phone calls were returned, no one would give his name or the name of the group. I realized with horror that the paranoia that had begun to destroy my classmates had rooted itself in the very community that needed to protect itself the most. Disappointment followed disappointment as I discovered that the group for teenage homosexuals in Philadelphia no longer existed, that one group wanted only Hispanics, another Catholics, another men twenty-one and over. It seemed to me that the more I wanted to free myself from the shackles of conventional thinking, the greater my struggle.

I heard about Cooper River Park, a cruising ground, and thought maybe I could meet someone there. I remember being afraid of someone talking to me, and afraid of no one talking to me. But here was something I felt I had to do. I got out of my car, put my hands in my pockets, and walked casually down the street. A few men stared, and a couple cars turned around, but not one person said a word as I walked by, my heart pounding loudly. Not one person, not one word.

As I returned to where I had parked, I noticed that a lot of guys were still in their cars, just sitting there in the darkness, occasionally turning on their lights inside so I could see what they looked like. It was a meat market, not a meeting ground.

I can't express how painful it was for me to see. Was this how I would end up, so degrading, so dehumanizing, so impersonal? I imagine they were all looking for sex, but none were brave enough to leave their security for it. How odd it all was to me, a sheltered brat from Cherry Hill, who was willing to take a chance! Here were all these guys, far more experienced than me, and far more afraid. Probably more afraid of rejection than of being found out, I suspect.

These cars were nothing more than portable closets in which the men could hide in the dark. When they occasionally saw someone they were willing to risk opening up for, they would turn on their lights like a boy peeking out from the closet door, but never really ever coming out of it. Depressed, I drove home alone. No one ever spoke a word to me there. The silence that haunted me at school was everywhere.

I finally found a support group that would have me, and I'm making every effort to fit into it. I remember going for the first time, half expecting a leatherman or a Judy Garland impersonator to greet me at the door. But it was just a person. And finally in this strange new place, I felt at home.

I was greeted cheerfully, and felt strangely at peace with these guys who talked about looksism, male lovers, and hair mousse, not necessarily in that order. It was the first time I was ever in a room with confirmed homosexuals and I loved it! The men of Men in Transition appreciated me because I was innocent and inexperienced, and I liked them because they weren't. Finally, the spell was broken. This boy who had lived a lie, if he had ever really lived at all, was really coming to grips with himself. I think I am doing a good job.

It is not in my nature anymore to be effeminate. I do realize, however, that I am now too bottled up inside. I'm trying to break down my defenses, though, to let down my masculine facade now and then; to just be a real person. It's not even easy for me to go outside without a tie on. But I do try. I'm taking lessons on how to throw back my arms, snap my fingers, and say, "Whoaa, girl!" The names Mary and Louise don't come to my lips so easily, but who knows, maybe someday they will.

Anyway, with support from family and friends, I'm a stronger person now. I've learned a great deal about people, about life, and about myself. I can accept myself for who I am, and I am making others do the same. I may always be censored, as I was in school, but I won't be silent. I can't be anymore.

My life exists beyond Cherry Hill and South Jersey, and, yes, beyond Cooper River Park and Gatsby's, too. I know now that life is more than manicured lawns and streets named after racetracks, forest animals, and brands of peanut butter. I know that being gay is quintessentially the most difficult road to travel. I've had to knowingly break my parents' hearts and learn an entirely new way of looking at life. But I'm not as scared, walking down that route, now that I know there are others there as well. And finally, I'm not only interested, but actually ready to discover it all.

Jeffrey N. McMahan

The Roundabout Way

My "coming out," or at least the great revelation to my parents, came later than I had originally hoped for. I had planned to tell them when they visited me way back in 1984. I had spent most of their last day (why "ruin" their vacation?) gearing myself up. Then, mere moments before I was going to open my mouth, in walked a neighbor, who remained ensconced on the sofa until I had to take my parents to the airport. The idea of telling them in a car, on a busy six-lane street, seemed a bit precarious to me. They flew back to Ohio without a clue.

And I had spent such effort to prepare them for the news. I had introduced them to everyone I knew, gay and straight, so they would see that I had a pretty good life with really incredible friends. I had forced them to watch *Brothers,* the cable sitcom about the football star, construction worker, and gay younger brother. I had, in a sense, set the stage – all for naught.

Over the next few years, I procrastinated. My trips to their home always seemed tumultuous – my mother and I can't spend more than a week in the same house without a major battle. Then, in 1987, on Christmas Eve no less, I decided to give my father the word.

Old Dad was pretty cool with the news. I don't think he was all that surprised. No screaming, shouting, or general scene making, just a simple "Well, I wondered," followed by "We can't ever tell your mother," and "Do we have to tell your sisters?"

I rather thought the idea was to tell *everyone*.

But with a little contemplation, I began to realize that Christmas would be quite the treat were my mother to find out. To put it gently, she has a bad history with "bad" news. All in all, I began to think that letting my father a step farther into my life was an accomplishment for which I could pat myself on the back. I left it at that.

The following year came news that my first book, *Somewhere in the Night,* was to be published by Alyson Publications in October 1989. Here was a new wrinkle, especially since, as my elder sister later put it, my real name appeared on the cover "in big black letters." In spite of widespread concern that I was publishing gay material under my real name, I could not keep this news under my hat. I had worked at writing stories and novels since I had been twelve or thirteen. I had to share the ultimate fulfillment of my one dream with everyone I could — and that meant everyone in my family.

Upon hearing the news, my father sat very silent a moment, giving me that dark McMahan stare. Then, in a moment of parental protection he would later regret, he announced that he should pass this piece of news along to my mother and sisters. In a way, he did: he told them all that his only son would be having a book published. But when he described the book, he only mentioned horror stories, neglecting to insert the all-important "gay."

That, need we guess, was his mistake. My mother, in spite of her continual lack of enthusiasm for my writing ambitions, began to tell everyone and their cousin about my forthcoming book. People were excited! "Horror stories, oh, Elaine, I *love* horror stories and will pee my pants if I have to wait too much longer to read Jeffrey's!"

Yeah, right. More than likely, Elaine will soak hers when she finds out exactly what kind of people inhabit Jeffrey's little tales of terror.

October 1989 approached with accelerating velocity. Here in Los Angeles, I wondered where it would all end while back in Ohio, my father assured me that he would take care of everything. No problem.

I reiterate — yeah, right.

Sometime in August I received a phone call from my younger sister. Dad had finally fumbled the ball and was waiting for someone else to take it home, and in such a roundabout way that I was hard put not to chuckle in Liz's ear.

Liz was eight months pregnant, and her baby shower had been the week before. In my elder sister's living room, surrounded by mother, sister, aunt, cousins, and various friends, Lizzie opened the odd sleeper, bottle warmer, and jumbo pack of Pampers. Downstairs in the family room, my father and two brothers-in-law drank Bud Lite and watched Sunday afternoon baseball. Sometime between innings, my father decided to spring the news on my brothers-in-law. "You know, Jeffrey's written this book, and well, he's kinda gay and so is the book, and do you think you could tell Gena and Liz, then we can all figure out how to break the news to Elaine, since she's telling everyone and their cousin..."

Can you picture it? I could, all too vividly.

My brothers-in-law are good sports; they passed the word on to Gena and Liz. Phone calls ensued, my father no doubt hiding somewhere while spilling his guts over his inability to tell my mother. By the time I got my call, I was the big boy who needed his papa to make things right.

Which, as far as Liz was concerned, was the only problem. For a born-and-bred Ohioan, Liz is pretty progressive. She believes we're born with our sexuality, whatever case it may be, and that part was fine and good and no trouble. The trouble was that my father was panicking and she, along with my elder sister, had decided I should bail him out before he worked himself into a complete and irrevocable tizzy.

I didn't panic; I was an adult. Wasn't I going to do this myself from the start? Good old Gene was the parent with the protection complex. I was — well, old enough to handle this on my own. I sat down and, after several days and profuse sweating, hammered out a letter to Mama and mailed it off.

I went back to my regular life, listening for the telephone with only one ear.

The phone didn't ring, but did I get a letter!

My mother, in her wisdom, decided to bear this burden *alone*. "We can't ever tell your father — do you want to give him a nervous breakdown a year before his retirement?" and "Do we have to tell your sisters?" They have small children, don't you know.

All right, call me callous, but I was on the horn, reading this poor deluded woman's letter to everyone I know. The laughs we shared — it would kill her if she knew!

But if one can't have fun at one's parents' expense, then at whose? I ask you.

The biggest question in my mind, however, was: Didn't these two people who had been married for nearly forty years ever talk to each other — at least about their children?

I do have some mercy in me. I called my mother the first thing the next morning and informed her that Dad already knew. I didn't tell her that he'd known for two years. That would have been unforgivable. She made a last-ditch effort to spare my sisters — they have small children, you know — but I had to nip that one in the bud, too. They knew, my brothers-in-law knew, even my nieces knew — they aren't that small.

But it was done, all out in the open and aboveboard. Of course, Mother's friends might wonder why the excitement over the book petered out so abruptly, or why she looks so uncomfortable whenever I visit and someone mentions "girlfriend" to me. Well, honey, I got girl friends, but would your blue hair go white!

That was all four years ago. At least my younger sister and my two brothers-in-law have read my first book. My elder sister is a sissy and couldn't handle it: "Fine, be it, don't write about it!" I took back a copy of the second book on my last visit but haven't heard whether or not it made the rounds. When I mention writing to my mother, I receive a long moment of silence. Imagine: writing, the great sin!

My father, on the other hand, has become an enthusiastic supporter of my efforts. He was quite proud when I received the Lambda Literary Award for *Somewhere in the Night,* even more so when *Vampires Anonymous* became a best-seller and went into a second printing.

Of course, no ending in real life is perfectly happy. My sisters don't think my father can handle the content of my work — meaning, the allusions to gay sex might mentally maim him. When I sent a batch of reviews for all to read, my mother confiscated them. My father doesn't have the nerve to ask where they are. He may support my writing efforts, but he still doesn't want to broach the subject with his own wife.

So this tale has no end. My part in this roundabout coming-out drama has expanded to educator — sometimes calm, sometimes impatient — but relentless, until the day when my family can talk about my life as naturally as I live it.

John Primavera

Welcome Nowhere

January 1972: "You should toy with the idea of studying law," my first therapist suggested.

"I like reading D.H. Lawrence," I answered.

"Try for a degree in history," he countered.

"But Walt Whitman is my idol."

"Be serious, John," he said in all seriousness.

"I am. Tennessee Williams wrote six hours every day."

My therapist winced. *John Primavera,* he must have thought, *a no-good.*

I was a sophomore in college when my rehab counselor sent me to this square, who wore a goatee trying to be hip. It only succeeded in making him seem pretentious. I remember hoping his daughter, who stood framed in a family portrait on his desk, grew up to wear a moustache.

People were always trying to steer me in their direction. When I was seventeen, and still walking, another counselor wanted me to go to accounting school. My first sex partner accused me of running to tell the teacher because I didn't want him pawing me. I fled in one piece.

One person who didn't try to pressure me was Bob. He was a deejay who hosted this fantastic gay radio talk show. He filled me in on what being a gay male was all about. He and the other guests would talk the kind of talk that was to be found nowhere else.

I guess I loved Bob and the other men on the air. He was the closest thing I had to a role model and hero, if you can have a role model at the age of twenty-eight. When I first called in, I had been in my chariot for four years. This man had a sexy voice, and kept turning me on, even though I had no idea what he looked like. I never mentioned I was in a wheelchair, just that I was this shy guy living at home, and was I doing wrong by leaving my *After Dark* magazines where my mother could see them?

He said that was okay, and made me feel free as a bird. Then he said I should be ready to explain to her why I liked magazines with pictures of naked male ballet dancers if she asked. "Mom," I fancied myself saying, "I like the dancers because they are so free and beautiful; so alive and healthy in a way that I am not."

She never asked.

Bob was a great host, and he often did naughty things on the air which got him into trouble, like groping guests while interviewing them. This creative use of the airwaves did wonders for the scared who needed reassurance, the shy and reclusive, and the unenlightened who were buried alive under tons of heterosexual conditioning. Listening to Bob was like finding an oasis in the desert.

One day I convinced one of his guests to come up and give me a lesson in going all the way with someone – which I hadn't done until then. When I wanted a repeat visit, he told me to start a gay and handicapped group, which I felt smacked of segregation. I told him what he could do with his advice.

I was destined to meet a long line of snobs who were much too freaked out by my chair to see me as their equal. Even my first lover, my Devil, was just another variety of snob who treated the afflicted with a different attitude. These artificial types never seem to remember their outcast role in society, and will put me down for not being physically healthy like they are.

◆

I am John Primavera. When I was seven, my older sisters would entertain their girlfriends by throwing off their shoes to boogie woogie, hug each other, and giggle about boys they knew. They'd have pajama parties where they would look in the mirror and change their appearance with paint. My brothers would entertain their buddies like men, which meant sitting on the living room couch, with wide spaces in between, and listening to the Yankees hit home runs. Now shake my hand firm and buy a jalopy wid me to show da whole block who is king.

◆

July 1952: We lived in a neighborhood that by today's standards would probably be called a slum. Back then we just thought of it as a city block up in the Bronx. Our neighbors were mainly working-class Italian and Irish, and I was a part of them since my mother was Italian. My father was Czech. Since my affliction was some years off then, I wasn't caged in by four walls. I roamed the streets, parks, rooftops, empty lots, and fire escapes of my neighborhood. Living among a lot of lusty Italians, there was always excitement, plenty of music and laughter, plenty of celebrations.

And there were other kinds of excitement: the games, the gang battles, stealing and defacing property. Being in a gang meant that you were always trying to overpower a rival or

174

impress another kid in your gang. We had lots of chances for close physical contact: a lot of wrestling with other boys. Since things were organized by age and size, you never had to worry about being at too great a disadvantage. The match ended when somebody cried "uncle," and I always delayed it to savor the warmth of the other boy's body, and the feel of his muscles gripping me.

What was more exciting about these activities was that no matter what, nobody ever squealed on anybody. So there was the possibility that you could pair off with a kid you liked, or had subdued once, or was a member of your gang, and go off together and do things. Since your kid was a "safe" kid, opportunities for sex came up.

There were gimmicks we would use to arouse one another, like talking dirty about girls. Another was to play out in the rain or snow so you would have to go into one of your houses and change into dry clothes. We would go down on one another, or jack off. You did this stuff anywhere. Maybe under a bed or in a closet, inside a cardboard box or in an empty lot in the tall grass.

You did this sort of thing until you were thirteen or so, then you got serious with girls and dropped your special pal. For those of us who didn't, there was the street corner society where you hung out being macho, until the opportunity for sex came and you could drop the act.

For me, this male bonding began to recede at age fourteen, when I developed a disabling condition. I drifted into pornography – usually male physique magazines from Sweden or Germany – and relied on fantasies of the "old days," when Tony or Kevin invited you over to watch them lift weights, got you to feel their bulging biceps, and then got into hot and heavy sex.

◆

"I'm new here. Is the music always this loud?"

"Sure, always," he coldly says.

"I really came to talk since I'm not in the right shape for dancing."

He makes no response, just gives me an embarrassed grin. So I move on. I hope the restroom is big enough for me.

"Ya really know how to whiz around in that thing. I have an aunt just like you," says a dude who is kind enough to pass my drink down to me.

"Yeah," I answer. Does he really think I'm like her?

"Yeah, she got one of them electric gizmos. Goes everywhere."

I smile and move away with my drink between my legs so it won't spill. I spot a dude giving me a glance and hope he's not doing it because I remind him of his uncle.

"You're nice," I say to a guy I think I might get somewhere with. "How about leaving together?"

"Love to ... but I gotta be up at six in the morning."

I always meet people who have to be up early or have a bad cold or suddenly remember they're with someone after they've talked with me for an hour. I've got all their excuses categorized. I especially like the ones who have a lover they want to get back with, and so they're being careful:

"We don't have to let him know, just let it be a secret between you and me."

"Oh, but you don't understand," he says almost indignantly, "I made a promise to be faithful."

I sometimes tolerate a drunk or two, since it's better than nothing. I wish I'd meet someone who'd just come out and say, "Sorry, I'd rather not."

◆

May 1973:

> Dear Mr. Primavera,
>
> I am sorry, but it appears our dating service doesn't
> have the facilities for someone with your special needs.
> Find your check to us in the enclosed envelope. I hope
> you will seek out opportunities in the ad section in
> which you saw us advertised.

The want ads? The nearest post office is twelve blocks
away.

It' s time for another therapist. This time he's gay.

"Patience," Dr. Lang says, "you've got to have patience,
John." We see each other every Wednesday. "I know you're
depressed at not having a lover at the age of thirty-one; but
while that may be crucial to your happiness and well-being, we
must work on other areas such as self-esteem."

For six weeks, I listen to his meditation tapes. I listen at
night and drift off to sleep hearing Dr. Lang's voice. I think I'm
falling in love with him.

"Now that you're halfway through college, what are your
plans when you graduate, John?"

"I'd like to be a writer. I'm thinking of working for a
publishing house where I could work my way up learning the
book business."

"You've seen too many movies."

"I know, Doctor, but it's what I want. I feel I need to be in
that world. I need that kind of stimulation."

"You know those jobs are very hard to find."

"Dr. Lang, I want to fix up my emotional life first."

"Yes," he mutters, "of course ... and we must naturally see
to that as well."

177

One day about a month later he's discussing *his* sex life with me: "We met in this posh restaurant and then went up to his place. The next day we went off to ski, and afterwards in his cabin, we screwed all night. In the morning he made delicious scrambled eggs for me and we showered together."

"Wow," I say, "all that from just eating in the right restaurant!"

He laughs. He's in his shirtsleeves, and the sun is shining on him.

"Now, John, we must get back to you."

"But, Doctor, I love hearing about your love life."

"I know; but that doesn't seem to help you, and that's what were here for, after all."

I lean forward. "You're giving me glimpses into a world unknown to me, a world I only think of as fantasy."

"Living vicariously is not recommended treatment, John."

I feel like puncturing his grave demeanor. "Why don't you ever have me lying down? I told you our first day that I can think better and am more relaxed lying down."

"That's old-fashioned."

"This office is too sterile, and your nurse too starchy."

He tries making more excuses. But I won't let him get out so easily: "I feel like coming here was a mistake. I feel I'm wasting my time ... I'm in love with you."

He stops rocking in his chair. "I'm sorry about that." He ends the session. End of therapy.

◆

July 1975: I've been out of therapy for a year and have only six months left of college. In that year I've had mostly one-nighters or been used by men I didn't respect. I was slumming. My current roommate was a gay kid who needed a place until he found one of his own. He volunteered for the Switchboard, a gay clearinghouse, and one hot summer night he called me:

"Hey, John, I have a guy here who needs a place for the night."

"What's he like, Vic?"

"He's twenty-three and has red hair. Born in Wisconsin and his name's Danny. I told him you were my roomie and all that."

"Okay, bring him back with you tonight."

Danny arrived needing a bath. He got one, plus a tuna sandwich — which he ate on my bed wearing only a towel. I never got a pickup so easily, and never one who would need to spend the night. He was my first redhead. Chubby and kinda cute. He smiled shyly and we bedded down snugly together. I felt I could trust him, and I had no better prospects ... but after a week he was weighing heavily on my finances and took off. He called a week later to say he had a guy I would like to meet. Being curious, and alone as usual, I gave in.

David was different from Danny, but equally poor. David came from Boston and loved the discos. Danny was his pimp, I gathered, but all he got was a meal and the floor to sleep on. This was too much for my roommate, and he moved out. Danny got his bed and David and I slept in mine. But Danny could see I wouldn't tolerate David for long, so two nights later he came home with the Devil himself. Rick Olson made an impression.

"I can see ya need help, with no roommate and no steady."

"You talk so smooth and nice." *So handsome and blond,* I thought.

"I fuck nice, too."

He didn't have to sell me on it. Something clicked the moment he walked through the door. For ten months he stayed, and when it was all over he left a hole where my innocence had been, replacing it with a cynicism that would be permanent.

But Rick Olson, no matter what else he did, caused me to grow up. "Ya need to get out more," he said to me one bright morning. "Get up, lazybones." He threw off the covers and we went out for what was to be the first of many long walks. I had never seen so much of New York as I saw that summer. All the people and places had a golden glow, as if a hidden power were emanating from them. For once I was part of the scene, and not just occupying a space. I wasn't lowering my eyes as I had been, not avoiding life like a cripple, but experiencing new streets, new vistas, new sensations. For the first time I entered a bar with someone the whole place knew was mine. I was in love! No longer huddled in the corner away from the action ... I was *there*.

It ended when I found out he had been lying to me and cheating on me. I forgave him once, but it didn't stop. He left one night and only returned a week later to get his things. I didn't ask him to stay, because if he had it would have been the death of my soul. No matter how twisted my body, I had to keep my soul unruined.

My friends said I had nothing to grieve over. Some even wondered why I knew him at all. But they couldn't know how he had touched me. Poor Rick; poor John ... neither of us in shape for winning the goal we had set out to win. My love's self-hate proved to be, for him, what my disability was for me: a crippling obstacle to his happiness and well-being.

◆

I have this dream, where on one luminous day all the Johns and Ricks persecuted for their love will run through the sands of a golden beach, undespised and uncrippled. Above them is a brilliant blue sky, and before them the outstretched hands of the gods inviting them home to embrace and favor them.

Steven Corbin

Queer Empowerment

'm the only one like this ... There's no one else in the world like me...

This was the mantra I swirled around my not-yet-fully developed eight-year-old mind. Even then, I knew I was queer. With cute African-American and Puerto Rican boys in my third-grade class to ogle, those who stirred something inarticulate within me, how could I not know?

I lost my virginity to a boy at age nine. I wasted no time. Always knew what I wanted. Pulled no punches about it. Made no apologies for it — a blueprint of the man I would later become. As a queer man among my contemporaries, I was an anomaly. It was something I had always embraced, even before I began to celebrate it, even when I thought I was the only one in the world like this. I am at a complete loss for an explanation as to why I implicitly, subconsciously, and unquestioningly accepted my homosexuality. Somehow, I miraculously managed to elude the shame, the low self-esteem, the self-loathing, and the subsequent surreptitious, closeted behavior as I explored the underground labyrinth of being "in the life." My suspicion, though, is that it had much to do with growing up and coming of age in New York, where, fortuitously, the movement was born.

My subscription to the notion of being "the only one" was short-lived, because I witnessed, early on, a mob of effeminate men and drag queens who paraded up and down the streets of my inner-city 'hood, from whom I would obviously, however inadvertently, take my cue. Little did I know that these were my premiere queer role models. They were faggots. But they were no-shit-taking faggots. And everybody knew it. These punks (as they were called in the 'hood) and drag queens were not to be fucked with. Some of them had spent hard time in prison. Others had done their time on the streets. The only crime they had committed was daring to be the loud, screaming queens they were. Their judges and jury were the families and friends and neighbors who shunned and disowned and abandoned them. Their wardens were any number of studs stupid enough to think that queers were easy prey. This was the first hard lesson for B-boys who erred in their belief that faggots and punks were synonymous.

These street queens were the predecessors of those characters whose lives we glimpsed, like voyeurs, in *Paris Is Burning*. Before Pepper LaBejia, Venus Xtravaganza, and Willi Ninja, there were Sweet Willie, Miss Cookie, and Curl Top. Watching and observing this subculture from a safe distance, unaware that I would be claiming it as my own in a number of years, I saw, even through the eyes of an impressionable child, that there were myriad possibilities. And as my mother, her cluster of sisters, and my grandmother sat within the safe perimeters of the front yard, with its rusty wrought-iron gate, surreptitiously ridiculing the Miss Things parading up and down the avenue in broad daylight, little did they know that a few of their own sons were either queers- or queens-in-training.

◆

I'm the only one like this...

Growing up gay is not easy. Growing up in the "ghet-toe" is even more difficult. And growing up queer in the inner city is a worst-case scenario, if not nearly impossible. Against my will, I was cast among my peers — young, robust black men, chests and egos swollen and inflated with their ripening masculinity, looking for someone they could bully, terrorize, humiliate, and, more importantly, upon whom they could sharpen their homophobic fangs. This was not a safe haven in which I could explore and search for my sexual identity. Consequently, queers — or should I say, *out* queers — growing up in this dismal and destitute milieu inevitably inherit a sense of how to do battle when necessary. We do not turn the other cheek or take homophobic crap lying down. That, coupled with the credo my mother nursed me on — Be afraid of nothing and no one; fear only God — would culminate and eventually explode within me, forcing me to be, in some way, to some degree, the in-yo'-face fag I would become by my teenage years. An alchemy not to be underestimated or tampered with.

Nearly all the African-American, Puerto Rican, and Italian gay boys I ran the streets of New York with were like me. We took no shit: not from our parents, not from society-at-large. And certainly not from some young, heterosexist punk whose narrow ass any one of us could kick blindfolded. My coming-of-age memoirs recall a territory in the Village we claimed as our own, our turf, where outsiders and Other were no more welcome than we were within their domain. My formative years are bursting-with-living-color snapshots of sensual, humid summer nights that seemed to last forever, a plethora of beautiful natives and street urchins cooling off in the flowing, gushing rusty water of fire hydrants, celebrating our youth, our city, our sexuality. Straight boys were notorious for invading that territory, the borders of which clung, like a needy lover, to the outskirts of Washington Square Park and the concrete campus of New York University. These heteros, all full of their destructive male energy, were stupid and brazen enough to mistake us for screaming, cowardly queens who'd flee into the night no sooner than one of them called one of us a faggot. They were in for a surprise. Despite their weekly returns to vindicate themselves and to reclaim what they considered their "manhood," they learned the first night (as we would reiterate for them on subsequent nights) that we were not going to run away. Like them, we too were young boys from the streets, the housing projects, and the barrios, all full of our male energy, as well – however indisputably effeminate some of that energy was. So when one of the heteros invaded our space by jumping uninvited into our double-dutch rope (as we turned it frantically and chanted ditties – *Who is the boy that you love the best?*) we simply weren't having it. A fight broke out. Sometimes, a sprawling free-for-all. They learned, much to their dismay and chagrin, that ounce for ounce, punch for punch, we were not to be fucked with. We were not the easy targets they thought we were. We were kickin' ass an' takin' names.

◆

There's no one else in the world like me...

You can imagine my shock once I enrolled in a West Coast university, joined the formerly underground Gay Student Union, and met an overwhelming number of gay men and lesbian women who were not, by a long shot, the queer men and women I had just left behind in New York. I've since come to define the difference: gay is gay and queer is gay politicized. Simply put, many people, perhaps too many, are gay; they sexually conduct themselves as homosexuals among their friends, their community, and in the privacy of their bedroom. Once they cross that threshold and venture into the larger, hostile, outside world, they are gay no more. You know the type. You've met them before. They're the people who don't tell their family or anyone at work that they're gay because "it's nobody's business."

Queers, conversely, conduct themselves as queers whenever, wherever they are. Their queerness is not something they leave on the doorknob like a Do Not Disturb sign upon leaving their bedroom. Queers kiss openly in the street when greeting one another. Queers kiss their boyfriends, or their girlfriends, and hold hands when the impulse strikes them. Queers, in a business-as-usual manner, openly discuss and divulge their lives as queer people among the not-so-queer-friendly. Gay people allow themselves to be considered or presumed straight. Queers wouldn't have it. One of the most insulting things one can do to me is to presume I'm hetero.

Arriving at the campus of this big-time private university, thrust among so many of my decidedly gay, so-called peers, I was confused. Many of these people were gay *only* among each other. Once they stepped outside the Norman Topping Student Activities Center, they were gay no more. And don't dare even speak to them on University Avenue or in front of the statue of Tommy Trojan. Don't even think it. Sadly enough, I learned this lesson by doing just that. And I was so ignored by them on campus, so totally "dissed," that it irreparably shattered my naivete that every gay person was like me, that he or she celebrated his or her gayness in-yo'-face, as I had. But these were predominantly white, middle- and upper-middle-class students whose so-called best friends back home, nevermind their parents, didn't know who and what they were. These were people struggling with their sexuality, as we would learn during meetings and consciousness-raising sessions, and who had joined GSU, among other reasons, to guide and nurture themselves during their stumbling baby-steps of coming out of that dark, dank closet. I was attending GSU under the assumption that we could take our collective queerness, put forth an agenda, and empower ourselves on campus as such. But others were using the weekly meetings as psychotherapy sessions, whereby they were afforded the luxury of processing their Otherness and learning to accept and love themselves.

Boy, did I miss my New York queers.

Ultimately, I have always belonged to one or more sociopolitical activist organizations dealing with, and taking on, issues as they pertain to the oppressed in general, and African-Americans and queers in particular. Since age sixteen, I have marched for one cause or another, frustrated by having missed the advent of the '60s civil rights movement, of which I would've loved to have been a part. Yet I've marched and worked for everything from women's rights, civil rights, queer rights, AIDS activism, even clinic defense, whereby we vehemently fight the right-to-life fundies, bodily keeping abortion clinics open for women who want and need them. And I have found that my activism is, more often than not, focused on empowerment, whatever the cause. Thus, it is no mistake that I ended up in an organization like ACT UP, for instance. Political activism is the paramount expression and manifestation of self-love. When I take stock and inventory of my life and put it into some retrospective focus, I can clearly discern the pattern. By way of the rules and lessons I learned in self-assertiveness and, I imagine, because of the person I am, by nature, I've always lived my life out loud. As an African-

American, I deliberately, purposefully wear my hair in dread-locks since it is a manner of asserting my ethnicity upon a world that perpetually barrages me with, and shoves down my throat, the myth of the superior beauty of Europeans and their descendants. A culture that makes a point of negating my beauty, my history, my culture, and relegating me as Other — as in secondary and/or inferior. I wear and adorn myself with my queerness in like fashion. I want the world to see it, hear it, smell it, taste it, swallow it, dream it, as I've had to do with their hetero culture which acknowledges nothing and no one outside its narrow parameters. I am not an effeminate man and, consequently, must seek and explore other ways to manifest my queerness visibly, so the world makes no mistake about who or what I am. This is not a manifesto for others to incorporate and emulate or assimilate. But it works for me, always has, and I'm comfortable with it. My lifestyle doesn't exclusively celebrate my queerness during Gay Pride week-end, or at the bars, or in gay bookstores or coffee shops. Each day, I cherish and put forth my Otherness in one way or another.

And I know now, even more than I knew before: I am not the only one.

About the Contributors

Jim Baxter is currently editor and publisher of the *Front Page,* a newspaper for gay men and lesbians in the Carolinas. He's been publishing since October 1979.

Wilton Beggs was born in a rural area of East Texas in the family farmhouse. "My grandparents were the children of Confederates," he says. "I didn't know 'damnyankee' could be two words until I went off to college; I've learned a lot since then." Still a Southerner, Wilton now lives in Dallas.

Robert Boucheron is an architect in Charlottesville, Virginia, where he writes free-lance articles for local periodicals. He has also published fiction and poetry in the *New England Review, Hellas,* the *James White Review,* and many gay periodicals. At age forty-one, he lives in a renovated cottage with Cyrus, a cat. Hobbies include Greek and Roman studies and gardening.

John J. Carr was born in Chicago in 1920. Since his thirty years of seafaring ended in 1975, John has earned his B.A. and two master's degrees, as well as becoming very active in the San Francisco gay community.

Steven Corbin is the author of the novels *No Easy Place to Be,* an epic fictionalization of the Harlem Renaissance; *Fragments That Remain,* a tale about a dysfunctional 1920s African-American family whose eldest son is involved in an interracial homosexual relationship; and *A Hundred Days from Now,* a multicultural AIDS novel. His essays have appeared in *Genre,* the *Advocate,* and *Lambda Book Report.*

Wayne Curtis is a native Virginian who holds degrees from the College of William and Mary and the University of Delaware. Since the first edition of *Revelations* was published, Wayne has continued to write, contributing articles and reviews to *Gay Community News,* the *New York Native,* and *Lambda Book Report.* In 1989, he began his own graphic design and communications firm. He lives in Brookline, Massachusetts.

Larry Duplechan is the author of four critically acclaimed novels: *Eight Days a Week, Blackbird, Tangled Up in Blue,* and, most recently, *Captain Swing.* His work has appeared in the *Advocate,* the *New York Native,* and *Black American Literature Forum;* and in the anthologies *Black Men/White Men, Certain Voices, Hometowns, A Member of the Family,* and *Calling the Wind: Twentieth-Century African-American short stories.*

Thomas Frasier has lived in several areas since leaving Michigan's Upper Peninsula, including Indianapolis, north Georgia, central Tennessee, and Baltimore. He has written for the *Baltimore Gay Paper, Blueboy,* the *New Art Examiner,* and the *Advocate.* He recently moved to Vermont with his life companion to raise sheep, farm, and continue writing.

Robert Friedman started writing stories as a boy and has basically never stopped. He attended the writing program at Stanford University, where he wrote a collection of short stories, *Childlike Men,* and offered a class in gay male literature. His fiction appears in *Certain Voices* (Alyson). He lives in San Francisco, where he writes about arts and letters for the *Bay Area Reporter, Artweek,* and the *San Francisco Review of Books.* He goes by the name Roberto.

Mark Islam is a singer and songwriter who lives and works in Los Angeles.

Michael Lassell is the author of two volumes of poetry: *Poems for Lost and Unlost Boys* and *Decade Dance,* which won a Lambda Literary Award in 1991. His poetry has appeared in scores of journals, from *City Lights Review* and *Kansas Quarterly* to the *James White Review* and *Fag Rag,* and has been included in such anthologies as *Gay and Lesbian Poetry in Our Time, Poets for Life, High Risk,* and *Queer City.* His fiction and nonfiction have appeared in *Torso* and the *New York Times,* as well as in such collections as *Men on Men 3, Hometowns,* and

Flesh and the Word. A career journalist, he lives in New York City.

Vernon Maulsby is a poet and writer whose work has appeared in *Fag Rag, RFD, Philadelphia Poets, Gay Community News,* and in two chapbooks. He has also published a play. Since writing "Nightwings," he is older, no wiser, but more sensitive.

Jeffrey N. McMahan is the author of *Somewhere in the Night,* the 1989 Lambda Literary Award winner for Gay Men's Science Fiction/Fantasy, and *Vampires Anonymous,* a novel about Andrew the vampire. His work has been anthologized in *Embracing the Dark.* He is a resident of Los Angeles.

Steve Nohava graduated from high school near the top of his class. Currently he is in the honors program at Old Dominion University, where he is maintaining a 3.76 GPA.

Edward Powell/Zola is a professional female impersonator living in the Boston area. He has won the titles Miss Jacques, Miss DeRocco's, Miss Boston, Miss Massachusetts, Miss Gay New England, and Miss North Shore. He is also the show director at Jacques Cabaret, where he can be seen onstage six nights a week. His fans know him as the fiercest queen in Boston.

Scot Roskelley works in the public relations department of a Portland computer manufacturer and teaches college-level PR classes. Since writing his essay, Scot and his wife have concluded an amicable divorce. He is involved in a new relationship, and writes that he is "blissfully happy."

Don Sakers is a science-fiction writer and reviewer and has written three novels, *Act Well Your Part, Lucky in Love,* and *The Leaves of October.*

Adrien Saks is an activist and writer living in the Boston area. He is the co-editor of *Lavender Lists,* and his writing has appeared in *Gay Community News* and ACT UP/Boston's *Attitude.*

Guy-Oreido Weston is a freelance language specialist and journalist. His work has appeared in the *Philadelphia Gay News, Gay Community News, Blackout,* and *Au Courant.*

Laurence Wolf is a native of Manhattan who has lived in the Midwest for thirty years. A veteran of World War II and a grandfather, Larry came out at the age of fifty-nine, and has since been active in local gay politics.

Bert Wylen was born, raised, and educated in the Philadelphia area. He has been published in the *Advocate, Philadelphia Gay News, Philadelphia Inquirer,* and assorted other publications. In addition to his weekly radio magazine *Gaydreams,* he has produced features for the Pacifica Radio Network, as well as several nationally distributed radio documentaries, including *Unfriendly Fire: Lesbians and Gays in the Military* and *Give Me Those Moments: Parents Remember Their Gay Sons Who Died of AIDS.* He now lives in Center City, Philadelphia.

Alyson Publications publishes a wide variety of books with gay and lesbian themes. For a free catalog or to be placed on our mailing list, please write to:
Alyson Publications
40 Plympton St.
Boston, MA 02118
Indicate whether you are interested in books for gay men, lesbians, or both.